Praise for

*Total Alignment* takes Riaz Khadem's terrific ~~One~~ ~~~~
*Management* technique to the next level. It's a blueprint for
moving any organizational team forward towards
the greater good.

—KEN BLANCHARD, COAUTHOR OF *THE NEW ONE MINUTE MANAGER®*
AND *COLLABORATION BEGINS WITH YOU*

One of the leading causes of companies not achieving their
maximum potential is the lack of organizational alignment in
strategy definition and implementation. *Total Alignment* is the
answer to organizations achieving their potential and provides
lots of practical insight as to how to achieve this elusive goal.
Recommended to all managers, new or experienced, domestic
or international, old or new economy, everybody
can greatly benefit from it.

—JAVIER FERNÁNDEZ, MEMBER OF THE BOARD OF DIRECTORS OF CEMEX

This book offers a great step-by-step method that enabled
our company to spread our business model.

—DANIEL SERVITJE, CEO OF GRUPO BIMBO

For the first time we have a book that puts it all together:
management processes that have always been apart
are now aligned and integrated.

—HÉCTOR RANGEL, FORMER CHAIRMAN OF THE BOARD FOR BBVA BANCOMER

*Total Alignment* helps everyone in a company focus on what's
important and truly generates value, thus shaping a
collaborative culture within the firm. For us it has
been a culture-changing philosophy.

—GRACIANO GUICHARD, CEO OF LIVERPOOL DEPARTMENT STORES

*Total Alignment* gives us a solid framework to help an organization achieve high levels of performance. The concepts in this book are powerful and the beauty of lies in their simplicity, clarity and common sense.

—Roberto Montelongo, COO of Softtek, a global provider of process-driven IT solutions

We have implemented *Total Alignment* for nearly 20 years. The management technique helps companies go from vision to strategy, from specific decision making to execution of key goals which makes all the difference when steering your company towards your set targets.

—Jorge Ballesteros Franco, Chairman, GMD Resorts

This book is the Bible for any CEO looking for a management model based on employee accountability and empowerment. It helps you develop and maintain a new cooperative culture where each employee offers their commitment and individual contribution to the benefit of the whole company.

—Armando Muñoz, CEO of Sotec Spain

Well written, filled with useful, practical gems, without needless fluff, *Total Alignment* is perfect for the busy executive looking for quick, digestible knowledge that is equally easy to apply. A must read for leaders who seek to further evolve their leadership, operational efforts, and organizational effectiveness.

—Jenny Carrillo, VP of Account Management at American Well

Great contribution for the managerial community worldwide, independent of size and economic sector, to align and execute strategy with great impact on leadership style and organizational culture. *Total Alignment* should be mandatory reading to improve results.

—Hugo Estrada N., CEO of Remolina Estrada Consulting

*Total Alignment* is a methodology that helps you implement company strategies and improve personal leadership. It touches the most delicate borders between wanting to do something and showing you how things can happen.

—Zahie Edid, Director of Organizational Development, Liverpool department stores

*Total Alignment* has allowed us to survive through the most difficult financial times and crisis, and helped us thrive through a simple group of processes that helped align our vision for the years to come with complete and total accountability.

—Norberto Sanchez, CEO of Norsan Group

The *Total Alignment* methodology is the most exciting mechanism I have ever seen. Empowering the employee and the leader at all levels, this book shows you the benefits of having everyone in the company doing what the company expects using simple strategies to effectively manage the growth of your company.

—Javier Gorostiza, Director of Projects at SOTEC

*Total Alignment* is a complete system that helps organizations achieve vision and really live their mission supported by practical processes that guide the achievement of results. It integrates efforts towards the same direction in a surprising way and is an integral solution that greatly increases the chances of success.

—Antonio de la Llata, CEO of Grupo Guaymex Mexico

Riaz Khadem has developed a simple and effective framework based on what successful managers and entrepreneurs do in order to align everyone in an organization of any size. A must read for anyone looking to manage and direct groups of any kind looking to achieve long term goals.

—Juan Pablo Loperena, CEO of TIP Mexico

Now it's even more clear that this is a book that is not enough to read once or twice. It should be part of the team training in every organization. It's a great present when I mentor other entrepreneurs. It's amazing how *Total Alignment* can guide entrepreneurs to take their companies to the next level by having them focus on what is important in today's fast growing market and have a guide to make it happen.

—JORGE ARTEAGA, MANAGING DIRECTOR OF HOLISTIK

*Total Alignment* is a masterful work that integrates and aligns vision with the organization getting extraordinary results. Read this powerful book and learn from one of the best.

—OSCAR ODRIOZOLA, HEALTHCARE SPECIALIST WORKING WITH BENAVIDES CHAIN OF PHARMACIES, MEXICO

This book consolidates Riaz Khadem's decade-long experience with strategic management to offer a clear method of moving from strategy to implementation in an effective and lasting way.

—JAIME GARCÍA NARRO, NATIONAL EXECUTIVE EDUCATION DIRECTOR OF EGADE BUSINESS SCHOOL, TECNOLÓGICO DE MONTERREY

The book's description of lack of alignment in organizations is quite real and usual. *Total Alignment* is a good guide for addressing everything needed to achieve objectives and align the organization with its strategy.

—JORGE DEL POZO, DIRECTOR OF PRODUCTION OF BERLYS CORPORACIÓN ALIMENTARIA, SPAIN

# Total Alignment

## TOOLS AND TACTICS FOR STREAMLINING YOUR ORGANIZATION

Riaz Khadem & Linda Khadem

**EP**
Entrepreneur
PRESS®

Entrepreneur Press, Publisher
Cover Design: Andrew Welyczko
Production and Composition: Eliot House Productions

This publication is designed to provide accurate and authoritative information
in regard to the subject matter covered. It is sold with the understanding that
the publisher is not engaged in rendering legal, accounting, or other professional
services. If legal advice or other expert assistance is required, the services of a
competent professional person should be sought.

**Library of Congress Cataloging-in-Publication Data**
   Names: Khadem, Riaz, author. | Khadem, Linda, author.
   Title: Total alignment: tools and tactics for streamlining your organization
      / by Riaz Khadem, PhD and Linda Khadem, J.D.
   Description: Irvine, California : Entrepreneur Media, Inc., [2017]
   Identifiers: LCCN 2017002901| ISBN 978-1-59918-601-6 (alk. paper) |
      ISBN 1-59918-601-2 (alk. paper)
   Subjects: LCSH: Organizational change. | Organizational behavior. |
      Organizational effectiveness. | Management.
   Classification: LCC HD58.8 .K495 2017 | DDC 658.4/06—c23
   LC record available at https://lccn.loc.gov/2017002901

Printed in the United States of America

21  20  19  18  17                                                10 9 8 7 6 5 4 3 2 1

*"Blessed and happy is he that ariseth to promote the best interests of the peoples and kindreds of the earth."*
—Bahá'u'lláh

# Contents

# Foreword
## by José Antonio Fernández Carbajal*,
### Executive Chairman of the Board of Directors, FEMSA

T hanks to the dedication and the integration of a great group of people, the loyalty of our customers and lots of work, FEMSA has now grown to USD 19.4 billion in revenues with more than 265,000 collaborators. It is the largest beverage company in Latin America, the fastest growing and most profitable retailer in Latin America, and the largest bottler for Coca Cola worldwide. I had the good fortune to run this company as CEO from 1995 to 2014 and currently serve as the Executive Chairman of the Board of Directors.

When I was invited to speak about leadership at the Stanford Graduate School of Business a few years ago, they asked me to discuss my approach to leadership. Two things have helped me a lot.

The first was a lesson I had learned early on in my career from my father-in-law. He insisted that the key to success in our business was controlling our commercial agenda regarding the products we were selling in Mexico. It helped me understand that leaders must constantly understand and control the key operating factors of any project or any enterprise.

---

* named one of world's top 30 CEOs by *Barron's*

The second is related to the concepts in this book you are reading. When I became the CEO of FEMSA, a very important achievement was that I learned how to respect my team's decisions. I had to control myself not to impose decisions on my team. If you want someone who reports to you to be responsible for what he does, you can advise him, ask him, suggest to him, hint to him, but at the end, let him decide. Obviously, he knows that if he fails, he can be blamed and will be responsible. But if you impose any decision, you are first protecting him and, second, you end up being responsible for what will happen.

Closely related to this aspect of leadership are some concepts that have helped me as CEO of FEMSA in different stages:

- Encourage teamwork
- Focus on being people oriented
- Conduct strategic and deep analysis of situations and contexts
- Focus on long-term growth
- Exercise financial caution

These and many other ideas are developed in *Total Alignment*. I was fortunate to read Riaz Khadem´s first book, *One Page Management*, when I had just been appointed as the CEO of FEMSA. Riaz's company had been implementing the concepts from this first book at Bancomer, Mexico's second largest bank. After reading the book, I was eager to have contact with Riaz. We met in my office.

The process of alignment and transformation within FEMSA began with an offsite session of my executive team. We all flew to Houston, Texas. With Riaz's help, we reviewed our mission, vision, and values. We were captivated by looking forward to what FEMSA could become in the future, and were thrust into the process of analyzing how to reach that vision by adding more value to the organization.

We have now far surpassed the vision we had created with him: Employment has increased seven times; revenue has increased 21 times; EBITDA has increased 16 times; and market value in U.S.

dollars has increased 14 times when comparing numbers from 1996 to 2016.

Contacting Riaz to help us implement the concepts of this book in FEMSA was critical for our growth. We needed a unified language to be able to understand and measure our progress and we required full agreement on what were our critical success factors for each and every member of the team. Riaz helped enormously in doing that. He introduced the process of using his methodologies and solutions to transform the way we operated by forcing us to work as a team.

Our implementation of Total Alignment (known as TOPS at the time) took some time to be implemented, especially because we had to convince the team at the beginning; but now we all agree that it worked extremely well and that it helped us unify and align ultimate goals for the company, impacting positively several key factors: productivity, team work, flexibility and communication. Many concepts in this book you are reading including vertical review and critical success factors are now part of our culture.

Here are a couple of ideas for entrepreneurs who dream of turning their projects into a large company: First, know that your small business can become big. Big businesses often ignore small businesses, saying it takes as much effort to run a small or large business, so why bother with a small business. I say that a small business can become a big business if you put passion into it and organize with a great team. We did that with OXXO and grew it from 350 stores to over 15,000. Sometimes, it is even better and easier to make a small business large and create value. Second, what you need to do first, and forgive my insistence, is to form a great team. And to keep and develop a great team you need discipline, transparency, and communications. All of these can be achieved through Total Alignment.

Read this book from cover to cover. It will positively change your thinking on managing any kind of enterprise, project, or organization. The wealth of knowledge and experience put forth in it bolsters my already-high confidence that companies with great teams that are fully aligned can contribute to the well-being of the worldwide community, creating a lot of value and becoming truly great.

# Preface

There are times in life when a chance encounter is not by chance, or when events happen in a particular sequence beyond our control. This book is a case in point. It has a life of its own with an amazing story.

We went on vacation to Honolulu a couple of summers ago. We very nearly didn't take the trip because of our workload, but plans had been made so we went. We checked into a resort hotel but soon realized that it lacked some of the facilities of another one in the same chain where we had stayed before. We attempted to change our hotel, but the other one was totally booked.

After a few days, I changed my routine and decided to swim in the pool early in the morning. Trying to avoid the sun, I searched for a seat in the shade. Every chair had a towel reserving it except for one. I happily sat down and then realized that my neighbor was engrossed in a lively conversation that I couldn't help but overhear. It became apparent that she had just closed an exciting book deal.

When she finished her call and turned to me to apologize for talking loudly, I asked her if she was a literary agent. Yes, she said, wondering how I had figured it out. This opened a conversation in which I mentioned that we had successfully introduced the book *One Page Management* into the U.S. market several years back with the help of a literary agent. The book had been subsequently published in twelve countries. We then wrote a sequel that was doing very well in Mexico and South America but was not picked up by the U.S. publishers. Our former literary agent had passed on it. The name of that sequel was *Total Alignment*.

It turned out this woman was Wendy Keller, a highly successful literary agent with an incredibly positive attitude towards life. She asked to see the manuscript and read it on her return flight to Los Angeles. One week later, we signed a contract giving Wendy the right to represent us worldwide.

Through the summer months, this remarkable person, who has an amazing story of her own, guided us through every step of the challenging proposal process. She helped us prepare for the presentation of the book to the top U.S. trade publishers in September. By November, we had received a contract from Entrepreneur Press. They saw potential in the content and agreed to publish it. They recognized the value of the message and its appeal to leaders, and they asked us to also address the needs of entrepreneurs.

We began a research of the literature to understand more completely the issues that entrepreneurs face. And then another serendipitous event occurred. Suddenly and unexpectedly, I received a LinkedIn message from a former client I had not been in contact with for nearly 15 years. Norberto Sanchez, an extremely successful entrepreneur who had built a restaurant business in the Southeast from nothing to more than a $100 million dollar business, sent me a message inviting me to lunch. When we met, he told me that he wanted to give me a book that complemented the work we had done for him. A few days later, he sent me a copy of *No Man's Land* by Doug Tatum. Among all the books about entrepreneurs, this particular book identified the issues and challenges they face in a very meaningful way.

It is still incredible to relive the events that led to the publication of this new version of *Total Alignment*. The hand of fate has no doubt played a role, as there were too many coincidences for it to have happened by chance. The combination of events illustrates that there are times when "chance" encounters are not by chance, and that efforts to pursue a goal can attract breezes of confirmation.

# Introduction

The journey towards *Total Alignment* began many years ago when we moved to Atlanta. Through a combination of circumstances we were introduced to Fran Tarkenton, the former National Football League quarterback and Pro Hall of Fame recipient. Fran owned a consulting firm that helped organizations improve productivity through behavior management. When we met and exchanged views on how companies could be assisted to rise to higher levels of effectiveness, Fran saw a synergy between our approach and his consulting practice. He invited me to partner with him in a new company, Tarkenton Information Systems.

One afternoon, Fran called a friend, the CEO of Greenwood Mills in South Carolina, saying words to this effect, "I have this guy in my company with amazing ideas. He seems to know what he is talking about. I want him to spend a couple of days with you guys to visit your facilities at no cost. He will be talking to people, looking at your data flow and your processes, and he will let you know how he can help you boost your results."

I spent two days at Greenwood Mills, visited their plants, reviewed their processes, talked to supervisors, the quality manager, the plant manager, the VP of operations and the CEO. By the end of the two-day period, a proposal had emerged: streamline the flow of management information, focus each position on its measurable added value, systematize the focus of everyone, and follow up for results. The proposal was presented with the implementation timeline and cost on the third day and was sold immediately. Fran was amazed at the speed of this sale. He contacted other CEOs he knew and sent me for two day visits. Within a short period, we sold five implementations. During this time I kept noticing the overload of information that managers were struggling with. The idea came to me of putting all the facts managers need to know on just one page. That was the germ of an idea that evolved into *One Page Management*.

A couple of years later, I had split with Tarkenton and decided to form my own company, Infotrac, Inc. With the help of my wife, Linda, I began to write a book about managing with one page. My wife and I sat at the kitchen table and wrote the book. We contacted Bob Lorber and he agreed to be the co-author. He shared the manuscript with Ken Blanchard, the author of *The One Minute Manager*. Ken was intrigued and became a fan. The book, *One Page Management*, was published in the U.S. and subsequently in 12 countries. New clients emerged as the book was launched in country after country, and our consulting practice expanded to deliver implementations in the U.S., United Kingdom, Austria, Germany, and Mexico. We developed a companion software, TOPS—the One Page Software, to track the information.

As we implemented the concepts of *One Page Management* in many different sectors we realized the need for an alignment process. The three one-page reports helped greatly with the identification of factors for the individual. But what was missing was aligning the reports with the strategy of the company. This was the stimulus for *Total Alignment*. The TOPS software has evolved into a sophisticated, web-based tool that seamlessly makes alignment possible. It can accommodate companies with a few managers to organizations with thousands of managers. The alignment concepts and processes were developed and were closely integrated with *One Page Management*. The result is this book.

## WHO SHOULD READ THIS BOOK?

This book is for leaders and managers in organizations of all sizes. To best illustrate how the concepts work in real life, we chose to use a fictional case study based on our experiences with clients around the globe. The story that introduces the concepts is based on a group of larger companies because we wanted to provide you with a breadth of scenarios so you can see how the application of these lessons might play out in real life. However, the concepts are equally valid and helpful for a company with divisions or a small company of only a few people. The lessons can be tweaked to fit your own organization's needs and circumstances. As long as there are managers with people reporting to them, the processes presented here should apply. The alignment challenge *all* companies have is the same: unifying the organization to achieve a common vision and produce results.

The book will show you how to release the power of alignment, how to create unified action, and channel everyone's energy in the same direction to achieve the potential for growth. Our goal is to help you improve your company's performance by eliminating conflicting goals and redundant activities, streamlining processes, and enabling individuals to become more focused on delivering your company's unique value proposition. Through the lens of alignment you will be able to see opportunities for growth waiting to be explored. Showing you how to harness the unique power of alignment is the purpose of this book.

*Total Alignment* helps you to think about some fundamental questions that every company must answer:

- ➤ Who are we?
- ➤ What are our core values?
- ➤ What's our purpose?

➤ What do we do and why?

➤ What is our mission?

➤ What does our future look like?

➤ What is our vision of the future?

➤ How do we get to that future?

➤ What is our strategy?

➤ How do we execute?

➤ How can we implement our strategy?

➤ How do we stay the course?

➤ How do we maintain alignment?

We offer you a framework that will enable you to answer these questions, and the solutions we present are more than theoretical concepts. They include unique processes, practical methodologies, and easy-to-use tools. All of the processes you'll read about here can link together seamlessly to create Total Alignment in an organization, no matter where that business operates. Although cultures differ, alignment is of value everywhere. The need for alignment is universal.

See below what James C. Collins and Jerry J. Porras wrote in *Harvard Business Review* in October 1996. We believe it to be a timeless statement, true today as it was when it was stated:

> *Building a visionary company requires 1 percent vision and 99 percent alignment. When you have superb alignment, a visitor could drop in from outer space and infer your vision from the operations and activities of the company without ever reading it on paper or meeting a single senior executive. Creating alignment may be your most important work. But the first step will always be to recast your vision or mission into an effective context for building a visionary company. If you do it right, you shouldn't have to do it again for at least a decade.*

The alignment Collins refers to is no doubt more comprehensive than what we cover in this book, but it's a goal worth pursuing regardless of your company's size or location. To help you reach that goal, we are presenting fundamental elements of alignment we have found valuable in our own consulting experience. They include alignment with the market, alignment with vision, alignment with values, alignment with strategy, and maintaining alignment through time. Whether you are an entrepreneurial company striving to scale up or a large organization intending to simplify and increase your effectiveness, there are valuable takeaways here for you.

## THE BOOK FORMAT

This book has 14 chapters. Each chapter describes one building block of *Total Alignment*. We have written *Total Alignment* in a format we believe will give you the most value. Each chapter begins with a running fictional case study that is based on real-life experience. The companies in the case study are not real companies but the issues are real. They are an amalgamation of scenes from various companies and people we have encountered in our work. The story is intended to set the stage for the issue to be resolved, issues that are relevant to companies of all sizes.

With this format, we are striving to give you an interesting yet informative framework for exploring the concepts that make up *Total Alignment*. We are presenting the story to explain the processes of alignment. The content is intended to facilitate the understanding of the process, rather than suggest a specific course of action to be pursued.

We then review the learning points from the story in the "Align It" section and discuss the theory behind the solution offered. This will help you learn more fully the concepts of alignment. Next, you will see examples to help you apply the concepts in your own business in the "Apply It" section.

## TAKEAWAYS AND TOOLS

In addition to the methodology and processes of alignment, we are including some value-added tools to help you with aligning your own organization:

➤ An online survey for assessing the alignment status in your company. The result of this survey will show you opportunities for improvement in narrowing the alignment gap.

➤ A template for linking the key performance indicators and strategic initiatives in your company with vision.

➤ A template for assigning accountability to your people within your pyramid of responsibility, and defining individual scorecards for each person.

➤ A tool to identify core skills people need to succeed, and an easy-to-use evaluation scheme.

➤ A template for reviewing results from month to month and taking action on escalated positive and negative performance exceptions.

➤ A scheme for linking pay with performance

We hope you will enjoy reading *Total Alignment* and will discover the power of this approach to take your organization to new levels of effectiveness.

# CHAPTER I

# The Need for Alignment

L et's begin with the case study we mentioned in the introduction. This running case study appears at the beginning of each chapter. In this chapter, you will get to know Brian, the CEO of XCorp, a large and successful group of companies in need of alignment. You will learn what we mean by alignment and why it is so critical to the success of an organization.

## ➤ THE CASE STUDY ◄

BRIAN SCOTT, the CEO of XCorp Group, walked into a crowded conference hall in Chicago and took his seat in the front row. He was scheduled to deliver the keynote address. Brian had been invited to speak because of his success in turning around an ailing company during the previous year, as well as his recent acquisition of a successful high-tech start up.

When his name was announced, he walked to the podium and surveyed the large crowd. He glanced down at his notes and confidently launched into his speech. Brian spoke about the type of leadership he had provided as XCorp Group's CEO. He communicated his vision for the expanded organization and his forecast of industry trends. He explained why TechCorp, a newly acquired company, was the right fit for the XCorp Group.

When Brian finished, he opened up the floor to questions. A young woman in the sixth row raised her hand and asked how Brian was planning to integrate the culture of the entrepreneurial acquisition with that of the larger group of companies. "Great question," Brian replied. It was a good question and was right on point. Brian knew he had taken on some risk by acquiring a startup with a distinct culture, but it was a calculated risk with the potential of phenomenal returns.

As Brian answered the woman with an optimistic explanation, his eyes fell upon a familiar face a few rows behind her. He was happy to recognize Mark Wesley. Mark had been a trusted advisor to Brian when he had first become the CEO of XCorp and was struggling to turn the company around. Brian had affectionately given him the name "Infoman" because he had solved many of Brian's information problems.

Brian proceeded to call on other people and field questions. When his time was up, he left the platform and pushed his way through the milling crowd hoping to greet Mark, the "Infoman," but Mark was gone. Brian shook hands with a few friends and colleagues and then made his way to his suite on the executive floor. Entering the room, he saw an envelope propped up on the credenza. Inside the envelope was a note that read, "Congratulations! And best wishes for the challenge you've taken on." It was signed, "The Infoman." Brian smiled as he read the message from his old friend and advisor. Mark knew that Brian loved a challenge, even though he viewed it as more of an opportunity. Taking on a new acquisition was both.

TechCorp was the brainchild of Norman Evans, an exceptionally gifted and creative entrepreneur who had started the company 15 years earlier with little capital but great ideas. From scratch he had built up a $75 million business but then opted to sell. Brian wasn't sure why Norman decided to sell, but assumed that the company was having difficulty "scaling up" or moving from a successful startup to a high-growth company. TechCorp was still relatively small, but Brian could see that it had great potential. He had studied the numbers, done his due diligence, and then made the owner an attractive offer. Norm happily accepted. Brian was hoping that this startup would become a source of research and development (R&D) for XCorp and that it would complement XCorp Group's other products and services.

Brian was right. TechCorp was scaling up and had hit a stage many entrepreneurial organizations know all too well: a challenge with capital. Norm's vision was to move beyond the inflection point, the point at which a company is too small to be big and too big to be small, and become a major player in the industry. That vision, unfortunately, hadn't panned out. He had put tremendous effort into obtaining a source of funding that wouldn't cause him to give up too much control. But every source he had turned to insisted on securing the controlling share in his company. He had also researched and found a professional CEO whom he hoped would bring new energy to the organization and enable it to get to the next level. But Peter Bergman, the new CEO, hadn't worked out the way Norm had hoped. Peter had his own agenda and had made several bad judgment calls that had actually hurt TechCorp. Norm was on the verge of getting rid of Peter and looking for someone else when Brian Scott entered the picture and made him an offer he literally couldn't refuse. So, he sold TechCorp. He had a few twinges of regret, but mostly he just felt relief and gratitude for the excellent deal.

Alignment challenges with TechCorp began a couple of months after the public lecture where Brian had seen his old advisor. Suddenly, the new acquision lost its two largest accounts. Brian was concerned and wanted to learn the cause. He called the CEO, Peter, but found him evasive and unhelpful.

Brian decided to take a trip to the West Coast and visit the headquarters of TechCorp. After he arrived, he immediately set up headquarters in the conference room. He began his investigations by talking with Andrew Carlson, the director of sales. He was surprised and concerned to discover that despite a clear strategy developed at a planning meeting six months earlier, each area had continued to pursue its own agenda. The strategy was to focus on growing the core business, eliminating non-core products, and leveraging technology as the company's competitive advantage. To grow the core business aggressively, the strategy included implementing an integrated software system. It became clear that Andrew had not agreed with the strategy of eliminating non-core products because he felt they were still viable. To prove his point, he had continued pushing those products with existing customers as well as targeting new customers. Meanwhile, the sales people, busy promoting two of the non-core products, failed to spend time with important key customers.

The operations manager had fought to maintain the existing software system, which he had designed himself a couple of years before. So he passively resisted the new software and did little to support its testing and implementation. When complaints came in from customers about the software conversion, they were given excuses rather than solutions. There were also issues in marketing. The marketing people were promoting products the sales people were not actively pushing, thus creating expectations that were not met.

"All in all a rudderless ship," Brian thought to himself. He decided that the first step in getting TechCorp back on track would be to fire Peter, the CEO. Although it was a drastic measure, Brian could see that Peter was not working out. No doubt Norman, as he was struggling to get control of his business, had hired a CEO to help him manage and to put systems in place. This particular hire was a clear mistake. Peter certainly should have been able to prevent the loss of the two key accounts.

## ──➤ ALIGN IT: DEFINING ALIGNMENT AND ←── MISALIGNMENT

TechCorp shows an example of a company that has become misaligned. What does that mean, exactly? Think of it like a train that goes off the rails. The train still has momentum, but it's direction is unpredictable. For example, although a strategy had been developed, it was being ignored. People were following their own agendas with little regard as to what impact their actions would have on the success of the company. They were actively working against the strategy or passively resisting it. There seemed to be no coherent vision, and leadership was poor. These behaviors exist in many organizations (even in ones that haven't been recently acquired), resulting in a lack of focus on what really matters—serving the customers. But how do you determine if your company is misaligned? Let's first look at a picture of what we mean by alignment.

An organization is aligned when the following conditions exist:

- ➤ It has a unified purpose, a clear vision, and a strategy aligned with the vision.
- ➤ Individuals are accountable for their contribution to vision and strategy.
- ➤ Employees have clearly defined responsibilities supported by key information to track their progress.
- ➤ Individual competencies are aligned with team accountabilities.
- ➤ Behaviors are congruent with values.
- ➤ Teams at the right levels are empowered to develop and implement action plans to improve results. Cross-functional responsibilities are clearly defined, and spaces are provided for joint resolution of problems, so silos disappear.
- ➤ Compensation is linked to performance.

This definition describes the approach to alignment that aims to focus people within the organization on their accountability for the processes necessary to turn vision into reality and on collaboration across functions to continually improve the processes.

Here is our definition of misalignment. A company is misaligned when people pursue goals and agendas that are incongruent with each other and do not combine to effectively advance a single purpose. One way to determine the extent to which your company is misaligned is to watch for the symptoms we describe below:

➤ *Decision making takes too long.* Slow decision making decreases the momentum needed for growth and puts your company at a competitive disadvantage, particularly when you are competing with aggressive competitors and more agile organizations. There could be legitimate reasons for taking time to make decisions. However, if the slow pace is caused by lack of clarity as to who should make the decision, or poor understanding of the vision and strategy of the organization, then these conditions paralyze the ability to act and are indicators of the lack of alignment.

➤ *Too many meetings.* Meetings are necessary for exchanging thoughts and ideas, making plans, and reviewing progress. But many organizations are stifled by too many long and unfocused meetings that waste time and drain productivity. If this is the case in your company, the underlying cause could be lack of clear definition of accountability. When it is unclear who is accountable, then everyone is accountable and too many people are invited to meetings. In organizations hampered by a strict hierarchical culture, functional managers find it necessary to be present in meetings, or send their representatives to attend. As a result, meetings become too large and too long for effective action, and little progress is made when the meeting is over.

➤ *Overload of emails.* When we talk about the overload of emails, we are not referring to the overload of junk emails.

Those can be eliminated by your computer software. We are talking about legitimate emails that people receive and cannot ignore. Highly skilled, knowledgeable workers spend too much of their time managing emails. While important emails should be answered, a large number of emails are unnecessary. One main reason why emails are often sent in such volumes is because responsibilities are not clearly defined in many organizations and managers feel they need to copy a long list of people to protect their actions from criticism or to respect hierarchical protocols. Overload of emails could be an indicator of misalignment.

➤ *Silos exist.* "Silo" is a business term used to refer to departments working as separate units and not sharing information with other departments in the same company. The lack of communication may be intentional or unintentional. Functional units often become turfs that guard information and interests. Silos exist in organizations of all sizes. The story of TechCorp is an example of silos in a medium-sized company. The marketing department, the sales department, and the operations and IT department were all working as silos, not sharing information or communicating. The existence of silos is an indication of misalignment.

➤ *Lack of clarity of responsibility.* When responsibilities are not clearly defined, either no one is taking charge, or someone is taking charge who might not be the right person, or several people are fighting for control. These scenarios have varying effects on the bottom line of the company. When the results are good, then there is a tendency for people to compete to get the credit. When the results are bad, people could engage in finger pointing and assigning blame to each other. These are all symptoms of misalignment.

➤ *Lack of empowerment at lower levels.* If the lower levels in your organization don't feel empowered to make decisions, then you might be experiencing misalignment. The employees on the front line are the ones who sell the product, deliver the

product, and serve the customers. When they are not empowered to act and are merely waiting to receive instructions from
their managers, customers suffer and customer loyalty is lost.
This is an important symptom of misalignment. You want
your lower levels to be empowered with clear definition of
responsibilites, as they are your link to customers, with the
important role of helping your company align with the market.

➤ *Communication is selective to protect individual interests.* If
you sense that communication among people is not open and
free flowing, or if people are cautious about sharing information, you could have an alignment problem. Information is not
owned by turfs. It belongs to the entire company and should
be available to whomever has a legitimate need for it. When
a manager and a direct report converse, if the direct report
selectively shares information or hides information from the
boss, no useful outcome will result from the meeting.

➤ *Lack of motivation in the organization.* This is a general mal-
aise you find in misaligned organizations. It is the result of
multiple misaligned elements we described in the definition.
Lack of motivation leads to apathy, where people have the
attitutde of "whatever." Apathy is a serious condition that
can impact your success. It is the opposite of being unified in
purpose, having a clear vision and a strategy for success.

➤ *Confusion and rumors.* Earlier, we described what alignment
looks like in an organization. When that picture is absent, then
your people become confused as to where your organization
is going, what they should do and why. When people are left
confused for too long, many revert to gossip, sharing opinions and news that could become distractive or distructive.
Confusion and rumors are the byproducts of a misaligned
organization.

These symptoms are present in different degrees in companies
of all sizes. If you detect these symptoms, you may wish to explore
further the extent of misalignment in your company. We have

developed an assessment instrument that is described in the "Apply It" section below. It has been used with companies from less than $1 million in sales up to the size of $4 billion. It can help you prevent the type of issues that Brian discovered at TechCorp.

### → APPLY IT: ASSESS YOUR LEVEL OF ALIGNMENT ←

The assessment instrument we are introducing in this section has seven categories. We describe the categories and why they are important below. Further, we explain how specific chapters of this book help can you improve alignment in the category.

- → *Focus and direction.* This measures the degree to which the focus of your people is directed to achieve a unified purpose. Whether you are a small company or a large one, the people in your organization must be focused on delivering your vision and strategy. If they are not, they will focus either on their own agenda or other activities that will divert energy, cause confusion, and impede the progress of your company. What is the cost of lack of focus and direction? It is difficult to calculate an exact cost. But, for example, if 30 percent of the workforce is not aligned with vision and strategy, that 30 percent translates into 30 percent of your payroll that lacks focus and direction. This is a huge percentage of energy that is dispersed. Imagine the costs both in terms of human capital and actual costs that are incurred. But how do you focus people on the vision and strategy of your organization? You focus everyone by delegating the accountability for the elements of vision and strategy to the appropriate individuals at appropriate levels in the organization. This is explained in Chapter 6.
- → *Strategy execution.* This measures the degree to which your strategy is implemented or executed in your company. Strategy execution is the key to success and yet many organizations fail in this regard. According to business expert Paul Sharman, as quoted in Business Finance, nine out of ten businesses fail to implement their strategic plan: 60 percent build a strategy that

doesn't fit the budget, 75 percent fail to link incentives to strategy and 95 percent of employees fail to understand the organization's strategy. Failed strategies put companies at risk and damage their competitive position. The cause of failed strategies is poor execution. How can you align to improve execution of strategy? This is explained in detail in Chapters 4 through 7. Briefly, you define individual scorecards for everyone that establishes clear accountability for executing strategy. You provide training and support to help your people understand what good execution looks like, and you establish a systematic follow up mechanism. Monthly attention to scorecards followed by corrective action improves strategy execution.

➤ *Vertical alignment.* What you do reinforces what your boss does and what your boss does reinforces his boss, and so on. Does this apply to you if you have a small company? Absolutely. How can you detect a lack of vertical alignment? Here is a simple exercise. Write down five things your direct report must do to be aligned with vision and strategy and prioritize them by assigning weights to each. For example, out of 100 points, you assign a weight of 50 to the first because it is the most important, a weight 20 to the next, and so on. Then, ask your direct report to do the same for herself independently. When you compare the two lists, you will most likely discover a surprising extent of vertical misalignment. What is the cost of vertical misalignment? It could be huge. Although you feel your direct report is focused on the right things, the reality may be quite different. How can you improve vertical alignment? Through a management process we introduce in Chapter 12, called vertical review process. It is a monthly one-on-one coaching session of each manager and his or her direct reports to continually check alignment, and to coach the collaborator in improving his results.

➤ *Horizontal alignment.* This refers to cross-functional collaboration of people at different functions in the company. By arranging their agendas and spending the necessary time to support a peer to produce results, they contribute to the success of the organization even if the investment of time does not directly benefit them. Why is this important? This type of collaboration prevents silos from developing in the organization. The cost of horizontal misalignment translates to the cost of not completing activities on time because of the lack of cooperation. It also includes the cost of completing activities too quickly without the involvement of other functions. And, more importantly, it includes the cost of missing the opportunity of achieving a more excellent execution through the interchange of ideas and talents. How can you improve horizontal alignment? You can improve by embedding collaboration in the scorecard definitions for everyone. These concepts will be explored more in Chapter 7.

→ *Competency alignment.* This refers to making sure that the person who has accountability for specific indicators has the right skills and competency to deliver. Without it, delegation will not work, as the job will not be done with quality and the boss will have to take over or assign it to someone else. What is the cost of competency misalignment? If someone else has to do the job you are supposed to do, then double resources are spent to get the same result, not to mention the delay in getting the job done. Or the person without the needed competency does the work in an unsatisfactory way. How can you improve competency alignment? You can follow a process we present in Chapter 9 that suggests each boss and direct report identify and evaluate the skills the individual needs to match his scorecard. They develop and follow up a plan for improving competency in the skills. The plan might include further training, mentoring, or accompaniment needed by the collaborator.

→ *Alignment with values.* This means congruency of behavior with the values of the organization. It means applying them to the day-to-day activities of people in the company. What is the cost of misalignment with values? Misalignment with values gradually erodes the trust that your customers, suppliers, and employees will have in the business and culminates in the loss of customers, loss of suppliers, and even loss of talent in the organization. How can you improve alignment with values? You can use the twin processes we introduce in Chapters 11 and 12, team review and vertical review. Conversation about alignment with values takes place in both. In team review, the team discusses the application of the values to the work of the team. In vertical review, the boss and individual team member consult on how behaviors congruent with values are practiced on a daily basis.

➤ *Compensation alignment.* This is about rewarding people for the results they have achieved. When a person has added value to the company, he or she must receive a fair compensation. What is the cost of misaligned compensation? When people see that their hard work is not recognized, their motivation decreases. When people are rewarded based on an unfair system, you could lose your talent. How can you align pay with performance? We provide a mechanism for doing this in Chapter 13. It involves tracking all the metrics in the individual's scorecard and calculating a contribution index that shows the overall contribution of the person. You can use this index to determine the bonus and even the salary of your people.

### Using the Alignment Tool

The purpose of the tool shown in Figure 1.1 on page 12 is to give you an initial idea of how aligned your organization is. You are encouraged to validate the conclusions from this assessment with further data gathering and analysis. It is best to have a random sample of managers in your company fill this out rather than just the top person. That way you will have a more comprehensive view of people's perceptions. If you are a large organization, each department could be filling it out separately. If you are very small company, everyone could be encouraged to fill it out. The point is that the top

| Categories | Questions | Scale | | | | |
|---|---|---|---|---|---|---|
| | | 10 | 7.5 | 5 | 2.5 | 0 |
| Focus and Direction | Do people understand and accept the company vision and strategy? | Everyone | Most people | About half | Some people | Very few |
| Strategy Execution | Do all strategic initiatives receive the necessary energy to guarantee excellent execution? | All of them | Most of them | About half | Some of them | None |
| Vertical Alignment | Are people's goals and priorities, at all the levels, in line with the strategy of the organization? | Eveyone | Most people | About half | Some people | Very few |
| Horizontal Alignment | Are people collaborating freely with peers across functions? | Everyone | Most people | About Half | Some people | Very few |
| Competency Alignment | Do individual competencies match responsibilities for all jobs? | All jobs | Most jobs | About half | Some jobs | Very few |
| Alignment with Values | Are behaviors of individuals congruent with the core values of the company? | Everyone | Most people | Some people | Some people | Very few |
| Compensation Alignment | Is compensation linked to performance? | All jobs | Most jobs | About half | Few jobs | No jobs |

FIGURE 1.1 **Alignment Survey**

person or top team may not be in touch with the misalignment issues that exist.

You will note that this initial assessment instrument has one question for each category. For multiple questions, please go to our website, www.totalalignment.com/as. The score of 0 to 10 corresponds to your extent of alignment. If you get a score of four in a category, it means you are 40 percent aligned in that category. If you average all seven categories you will have an overall alignment index, a score that gives you an idea of the extent of alignment of

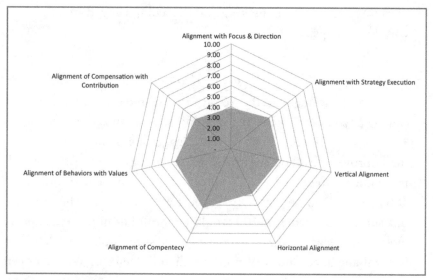

FIGURE 1.2 **Alignment Radar**

your company based on the seven criteria listed above. While this instrument is not a precise gauge, it provides valuable information.

In order to view your results visually, you may wish to construct a radar chart similar to the one in Figure 1.2, and display your scores on it. You can do this by drawing the radar and plotting the score for each category. If you enter your scores into Excel, the software will produce a chart for you.

As an example, the radar chart illustrates what a company with close to 50 percent alignment looks like. You will notice that the largest gap is Focus and Direction. This score indicates an opportunity for improvement.

The company illustrated in Figure 1.2 can typically be characterized as a company where people have not been involved in creating vision and strategy. Small- to medium-sized entrepreneurial companies where the owner pursues his vision, formulates strategy as he goes along, and makes all the important decisions would have a similar chart. Companies with a culture where functional silos exist tend to have a largest gap in horizontal alignment. Those companies that take the time and make the effort to include their workforce in decision making have a completely different chart with lower gaps.

### *Improving Alignment*

The overall average of the results in the radar is an index that can help you set a goal for aligning the organization. In Figure 1.2 this index is about 50 percent, suggesting a huge opportunity for improvement. You may wish to set a goal to raise the overall percentage incrementally to 70 percent, 90 percent, and eventually to 100 percent. Don't be surprised if you see low numbers when you use this survey. The score of 100 would be ideal, but in our experience, most companies we have assessed (even successful ones) have an internal alignment index of no more than 60 percent. We have seen companies with much less.

We encourage you to gather your team together, discuss the results of this alignment survey, and validate your findings with further data analysis. Find out if the gaps you have found accurately describe what is taking place. You will find the conversation to be extremely valuable. Once you have agreed on the extent of misalignment, you can refer to our description of the seven categories above to discuss the cost of misalignment that is imperceptibly impacting your bottom line.

## ➤ THE NEXT STEPS ◄

Now, we are ready to begin aligning your organization. In the next chapter, you will learn how to define a unified shared mission and vision, and why this is the fundamental first step in alignment. The chapter begins with a short continuation of the fictional case study to illustrate the key concepts related to mission and vision. In subsequent chapters you will learn concepts, methodologies, and processes to establish a solid foundation for alignment, to build alignment on that foundation and to sustain it.

# CHAPTER 2

# Unifying the Vision

B rian and his team members are struggling with something every company must address: how does the leadership team unify the entire organization behind its mission and vision? You will learn how to create a truly shared mission and vision and how to make them the cornerstone of alignment.

───────────────→ **THE CASE STUDY** ←───────────────

WHEN BRIAN SCOTT returned from his visit to the TechCorp headquarters, he contacted his trusted advisor Mark, the "Infoman," to discuss the challenges he was having with the new acquisition. In a breakfast meeting, they reviewed the TechCorp case and concluded that alignment was the main problem. The Infoman introduced Brian to the alignment assessment instrument, explaining the seven categories it measures and how it can be analyzed to show the perception of the people on a radar chart. Brian decided to try using the instrument at TechCorp and also in other businesses owned by the Group: XCorpUS, IES, and Cellular.

Based on the results of the assessments carried out throughout the group, Brian realized that not only TechCorp but also each of the businesses in the group were not aligned to different degrees and in various ways. The Infoman assured Brian that based on his wide experience, most companies face this issue. Of all the actions that Brian could take to improve alignment, the most effective one would be to bring his team together and involve them in an exercise to create a unified mission and vision for the company. Unity around these two documents is the foundation of alignment and would make any alignment initiative easier to implement. Brian agreed.

One month later, XCorp's top executives assembled at a resort hotel for a weekend offsite with Mark the Infoman. He greeted everyone and explained that the alignment process he was facilitating would be the key to reducing the gap they had discovered in their own alignment assessments. He emphasized that alignment begins with *mission*, *vision*, and *values*, and that these documents serve as the framework for linking all the activities necessary for success. He suggested that the participants could help him in the facilitation of the session by defining guidelines for consultation in their meeting consistent with an environment that was safe for everyone to contribute openly without fear of consequences. The Infoman proceeded to engage them in developing the group mission and vision. Below is the mission they came up with:

### Mission of XCorp Group

*Our mission is to connect people across the globe through instantaneous, high quality, and affordable communication.*

The vision that the group came up with is the following:

### Vision of XCorp Group

*Five Years in the Future*

*We will be the preferred communication company with a global footprint.*

*We will be distinguished from our competitors by exceptional quality and customer service, by the operational effectiveness of all businesses we own, our leadership in technology, the excellent and fair treatment of our employees, the outstanding value we provide for our customers, the satisfactory value for our shareholders, and our contribution to the community.*

## ALIGN IT: UNDERSTANDING THE ROLE OF MISSION AND VISION

The story you just read shows the executives of our fictional company coming together to create a common mission and vision for their organization. Each of the businesses within the group already had a separate mission and vision, but there was none at the larger group level. The value derived from the exercise was to create these statements at the group level by involving the team to assure ownership, understanding, and commitment to what they had created.

Most companies have mission, vision, and value statements as part of their business plans. They refer to them from time to time and might use them to motivate the employees, the investors, suppliers, or customers. Many display them on the corridor walls or post them by the entrance to their building or on their websites. But few companies place their mission and vision at the center of everything they do, linking all their metrics to mission and vision. For alignment to happen in an organization, this is essential. Mission, vision, and core values have to be front and center.

The core values of the organization are the statements of your fundamental beliefs. You would never break these values no matter how they might impact your bottom line. If customers don't like them, then you find other customers that do. You can read more about the core values in Chapter 10.

In brief, the three seminal statements, core values, mission, and vision, constitute the basic framework for alignment. First, let's have a closer look at the mission statement.

## *The Mission Statement*

The characteristics of an effective mission statement convey the purpose of the organization, not how you will achieve it. It communicates the value you are adding as a company through the products and services you offer. If the mission inspires your people, then they will find meaning in their work and will be willing to sacrifice their time to achieve it. It is the sense of mission that enables companies to grow and achieve greatness. Entrepreneurial firms begin with the mission of the founders and their dedication to turn it into reality. It is the power of mission that keeps them going through the ups and downs, the struggles and disappointments of growing the business.

There is much written about mission statements. Some suggest nine characteristics to be included in a mission statement, some seven and some five. The elements suggested generally include:

- Philosphy
- Image
- Products
- Services
- Markets
- Technology
- Profitability
- Growth
- People

We believe these are important elements, but far too many to include in the mission statement. If a mission statement becomes too long or complex, it loses its effectiveness.

In our consultations with clients, we recommend reserving mission exclusively to demonstrate the purpose of the organization: what the organization actually does and why. It is a statement that doesn't change with time. It carries you through years in the future.

Here are examples of the mission statements of four successful companies quoted by Jonathon Kervin, in www.Quora.com; by Andrew Thompson, in *Business Management*, updated September 20, and in *Science Alert*, on July 18, 2016.

**Uber:** *"to make transportation as reliable as running water, everywhere, for everyone."*

**Google:** *"to organize the world's information and make it universally accessible and useful."*

**Starbucks:** *"To inspire and nurture the human spirit—one person, one cup and one neighborhood at a time."*

**Tesla:** *"to accelerate the world's transition to sustainable transport."*

Let's look at Uber's mission statement. Its purpose is to make transportation reliable. When you visualize the reliability of running water downstream assured by gravity, then the image is vivid and useful. The words "everywhere" and "for everyone" show the intent of Uber to operate worldwide. You notice that purpose does not have to be achieved. Rather, it has to be aspired to.

In the case of Google, the mission implies that it does three things: organize the world's information; make it universally accessible; and make it useful. The implicit reason for doing these three things is to help people.

The Starbucks mission sounds good and is effective because it implies that drinking coffee or any other beverage inspires and nurtures the human spirit. If you love coffee, but disagree with the premise, remember that the mission is not for you, but for the Starbucks employees who are inspired to believe that this is the case.

Let's also consider Tesla's mission statement: to accelerate the world's transition to sustainable transport is an inspiring mission. It assumes that sustainable transport is inevitable and that Tesla can accelerate the transition from gas to electricity. What is implied here is that sustainable transport will become increasingly more affordable for people, will eliminate the reliance on oil, and also eliminate the adverse effect of oil consumption on our planet.

In the above examples, the reasons behind their mission are implicit, left to the reader's interpretation. However, the clearer the reasons are, the greater the power to inspire.

Basically, your mission statement includes

➤ What you do
➤ Where you operate
➤ Whom you are serving
➤ Why

Of these questions, the most important is the Why, because the answer to that question is your purpose, which is constant and changeless. You might change what you do or where you operate or whom you are serving. But why you are doing it will not change.

### *The Vision Statement*

Vision is about seeing how your mission is played out in the future. It is a picture of your future in five, ten, or twenty years. Clearly, the longer the window, the more difficult it is to visualize that future. Assuming that your mission statement addresses a fundamental need, the need will continue to exist with the passage of time, and while everything else changes, your purpose will not. Therefore, it makes sense to define your vision in 10 or 20 years. It is also fine to choose your window as three to five years, if you prefer. Regardless of your vision window, the vision statement conveys what your future looks like.

Let's look at the statement of vision in two of our examples above as quoted in an article by Andrew Thompson, in *Business Management*, dated September 20, 2015 and by Lawrence Gregory, *Business Management*, updated September 10, 2015:

> **Google:** *"to provide access to the world's information in one click."*

> **Starbucks***: "to establish Starbucks as the premier purveyor of the finest coffee in the world while maintaining our uncompromising principles while we grow."*

Take the Google example; their mission was to organize the world's information and make it universally accessible and useful. The picture of success of that mission is that people everywhere have access to the world's information in one click. You see how the vision statement is different from the mission statement, yet the two are related.

In the case of Starbucks, its mission was, "to inspire and nurture the human spirit—one person, one cup and one neighborhood at a time." The picture of success for Starbucks is to be the "premier purveyor of the finest coffee in the world while maintaining our uncompromising principles while we grow." Here again, you see how the mission and vision complement each other.

While the mission and vision are closely related, deriving vision from mission is a creative process that does not follow a linear path. It comes from seeing your mission succeed over time, considering the market needs, the trends, and the advancement of technology. We are not giving you a formula, only a set of questions that could stimulate your thinking as you attempt to visualize the future and arrive at your own vision statement. You should not copy the examples we have given above, or anyone else's mission and vision because your reality is different and the process of creating your own has inherent merit.

### *Quality of Mission and Vision Statements*

The measurement of the quality of your statements is the clarity they bring to your organization and the actions they inspire. If you want alignment, then our only requirement in formulating a mission and vision is that you engage your team in open and frank consultation to create inspiring statements—ones that your team is excited about.

The statements you create might be short or long or seem boring to those outside the organization. Don't let that bother you. It doesn't matter. The statements must have meaning for your team. They should inspire your own people. If the executives who created them are truly united and energized by them, then that's all that matters.

## ⟶ APPLY IT: DESIGN YOUR MISSION AND ⟵ VISION STATEMENTS

Let's apply the ideas of this chapter to your company and create shared mission and vision statements for your organization. As a first step, we recommend that you invite your team to a meeting, perhaps offsite, to spend a weekend to work together on this objective. Involvement of your people will ensure ownership and will enhance the quality of the final product. A skilled facilitator from outside of your team would be helpful.

### *Facilitating the Conversation*

When the team assembles, the facilitator gives an orientation on the concepts we discussed in the *Align It* section. Explain to your team that a good statement of mission and vision could have been crafted by the CEO and shared with everyone. That's one option for creating these statements. This, however, would not be a good start for alignment. The reason team members were invited to the meeting is to draw upon the knowledge, experience, and creativity of *everyone* in formulating these two important statements together. Not only will the end product have higher quality through their participation, but also the exchange of views will guarantee their understanding and ownership, two important factors in alignment.

To maximize the participation of everyone, we like to introduce a few ground rules for these sessions. You can collectively refer to them as "code of conduct." The facilitator should engage the participants by posing a question to them such as, "What guidelines do we need in order to create a safe atmosphere where everyone is comfortable to contribute?" The following is a recommended list:

- ➤ Ignore hierarchy
- ➤ Listen to understand, not to respond
- ➤ No interrupting
- ➤ No dominating the conversation
- ➤ No put downs or negative body language
- ➤ Participate without holding back
- ➤ Laptops closed and cell phones off
- ➤ Detachment from ideas and positions. Detachment implies not repeating or defending your opinion. Once a person presents an idea, it belongs to the group. If you are truly detached, you may even end up speaking against your own idea after receiving more information. Detachment allows the group to move forward and not get stuck on personal agendas or old ways of thinking.

The participants are more likely to follow the code of conduct because they have been involved in creating it. Assuming that your facilitator listens carefully and patiently to every idea expressed regardless of the person's position in the organizational hierarchy, then rich and meaningful conversation will ensue and your team will be able to craft a unified mission and vision. Be careful that you as the leader are the first to follow the code of conduct, which means not using your position to dominate or dictate the conversation.

Even if your company is small, the code of conduct will be very helpful in assuring the flow of ideas and building on them to arrive at meaningful conclusions.

### *Developing Your Mission Statement*

The first step in developing your mission is asking a series of questions. It is a good idea to project the answers on a screen so everyone can see: Here are the key questions:

1. What do we do?
2. Where and for whom?
3. Why do we do this? What is our purpose?
4. Does what we do today limit us in fulfilling our purpose in five years or beyond?
5. If so, how can we broaden the statement of what we do today?
6. What would be a brief inspiring statement describing our mission?

Once there is an agreement on Questions 1 and 2, you go to Question 3, which will lead your team to some social benefit your company is adding. Focus on that social benefit because that is your purpose. When you write out your statement, the "why" could be implied or explicit. Question 4 is meant to help you avoid limiting your mission to what you are doing at the present time. Conditions could change in the future and new opportunities could enable you to fulfill your purpose with different offerings. Reflection on Question 4 will help you answer Question 5 with a broadened statement of mission. The answer to Question 6 is your mission statement.

### *Developing Your Vision Statement*

In order to develop your vision statement, you should first decide the window for the vision. For example, is it three years, five years, or ten years? Suppose you have chosen ten years. The facilitator asks the participants to imagine the answers to the following questions in ten years' time:

- ➤ What does success look like?
- ➤ What have we achieved?
- ➤ What is our competitive position in the market?
- ➤ How is our mission succeeding?
- ➤ How is the advance in technology serving our mission?
- ➤ How are we demonstrating our uniqueness?
- ➤ How are we adhering to our core values?
- ➤ What would our stakeholders say about our success?
- ➤ If we were asked to write about our company's success, what would we write?

The answer to these questions can give you a list of ideas. The next step is to consolidate these ideas into a vision statement. A skilled facilitator would assist the group to combine the ideas, then prioritize and arrive at a brief statement that describes the vision of your company. Once everyone is happy with the vision statement, you can put mission and vision side by side and invite discussion of how they complement each other. The mission is the purpose and the vision is the picture of success in fulfilling that purpose. The form in Figure 2.1 on page 25 provides a guide for mission and vision definitions.

If the size of your team is very small, for example two to three people, this exercise can be done together in one group. If the size is larger, the quality of the end product will be higher if you break the large group into smaller groups, allow them time to discuss, and then come back to the larger group to consult on everyone's input.

Let's summarize the concepts described in this chapter. First, every organization needs three important documents:

| Questions | Mission Statement |
|---|---|
| 1. What do we do? | |
| 2. Where and for whom? | |
| 3. Why do we do this? – Our purpose | |
| 4. Does what we do today restrict us in fulfilling our purpose in five years or beyond? | |
| 5. If so, how can we broaden the statement of what we do today? | |
| 6. What would be a brief inspiring statement describing our mission? | |
| **Questions** | **Vision Statement** |
| 1. What does success look like? | |
| 2. What have we achieved? | |
| 3. What is our competitive position in the market? | |
| 4. How is our mission succeeding? | |
| 5. How is the advance in technology serving our mission? | |
| 6. How are we demonstrating our uniquenss? | |
| 7. How are we adhering to our core values? | |
| 8. What would our stakeholders say about our success? | |
| 9. If we were asked to write about our company's success, what would we write? | |

FIGURE 2.1  **Mission and Vision Statement Questions**

- ➤ Core values that describe uncompromising beliefs held by all employees of the organization
- ➤ A mission statement that describes its purpose
- ➤ A vision statement that describes what its future looks like.

We will talk more about core values in Chapter 10. We have given you some guidelines to formulate mission and vision in this chapter. We encourage you to assemble your team, develop these statements together, and then move forward in the alignment process.

─────────────────► **THE NEXT STEPS** ◄─────────────────

In the next chapter, you will learn how to measure your vision by defining indicators, thereby making it simpler to quantify where you want to take your company in the future. The chapter begins with a short continuation of the case study to illustrate the key concepts related to measurement.

# CHAPTER 3

# Measuring the Vision

The case study continues with the XCorp team in need of quantifying their vision in order to build the foundation of alignment. You will learn to facilitate the conversation and identify the important indicators that measure the intent of your vision.

————————————▶ **THE CASE STUDY** ◀————————————

THE XCORP VISIONING EXERCISE continued the following day. Mark, the Infoman, began the session by asking a participant to read aloud the mission and vision statements they had created. He reminded them that this was the solid foundation on which the alignment of their organization could be built.

He explained that the next step in the alignment process was measuring the vision. In order to proceed, first the vision had to be clarified. What exactly was meant by each of the phrases? The participants had varied opinions on the meaning of the words. The group then focused on coming to agreement on a clear explanation of each of the key phrases in the vision statement. After they held a lively consultation, they ended up with these results:

- ➤ *Preferred communication company with a global footprint.* Our company will be represented in major markets of the world, not every single country, but countries where we can be the preferred provider in quality, service, or price.

- ➤ *Outstanding value for customers.* The value we deliver to our customers is much higher than they expect. It implies exceeding quality requirements as well as expected standard of service.

- ➤ *Operational effectiveness.* The processes that deliver our value proposition to customers are working well and are continually improving to reduce costs and deliver higher value.

- ➤ *Leadership in technology.* We are the first to introduce the latest technology in our internal processes and in the products and sevices we deliver to customers.

- ➤ *Excellent treatment of employees.* The employee experience of working for our company is such that they would not want to work elsewhere even if they receive an incrementally higher compensation.

- ➤ *Satisfactory value for shareholders.* We are creating wealth for the company and our shareholders are satisfied with the return they are getting on their investment.

- ➤ *Contribution to the community.* We are careful not to damage the environment with our carbon foot print, we recycle waste, and contribute to the wellbeing of the community.

Having reached unity around these definitions, the participants then discussed what indicators could measure their progress towards vision in each of these phrases. The Infoman shared a set of criteria for the quality that was required in the indicators. Attention to the meaning of the vision elements and the quality criteria enabled the participants to arrive at an initial set of indicators.

## ──────➤ ALIGN IT: MEASURING VISION ◂──────

As mentioned in the fictional case study, the next step after defining vision is to measure it. To measure the vision requires a deeper understanding of what the words that you use to define it really mean. That is why you will need to dig a little deeper to make sure that everyone has the same understanding of each key phrase, so try to consult and reach a consensus about those meanings.

Next comes defining the right indicators that measure progress towards vision. Let's look at one of the statements from the story as an example, "outstanding value to customers." How can this statement be measured? How do you know when it is achieved? It must be based on solid evidence and not opinion. What information is needed to prove that this phrase from the vision is being realized? First, "outstanding" implies something that performs better than expected. How do we measure this? Two possible indicators would be one for quality and one for service.

Where do you find these indicators? You can either design a survey and ask your customers to rate the quality or the service of your offerings, or find the data within your internal processes from sales to delivery. The first alternative will give you the information you want, but might inconvenience your customers. The second does not take the customer's time, but only approximates the intent of your vision of providing outstanding value. An approximate measure of value delivered to your customers might be something like "percent repeat sales," implying that repeat sales come as a result of value perceived by customers. Or you can look at the "percent returns" assuming that a high percentage implies that the customer did not perceive value. We will talk more about the indicators for this and other phrases of the XCorp vision in the *Apply It* section.

Let's take another example. Suppose the vision of a pizza company is, "on time delivery." First, this has to be made clear before assigning an indicator to measure it. What is, "on time delivery?" It can be clarified by stating, "We deliver pizza within 15 minutes of the order." Now, you can define an indicator to measure this intent. How do you measure whether this actually happens? You can look at the delivery logs of the business and count how many times the delivery was within the 15 minutes as promised. A good measurement of this statement would be "percent delivered within 15 minutes." The measurement gives the owners of the company a clear indication of how their delivery service is operating. If their main selling point is, "delivery within 15 minutes," they would give attention to this indicator as their highest priority.

Here is another example to illustrate clarifying a part of a vision statement and converting it into a measurable indicator. If you state in your vision, "We will be the market leader," what exactly does this mean? Do you mean the leader in technology, the leader in ethics, the leader in customer service? If the intent of your statement is to capture your market presence, then your vision statement could be clarified by defining it as, 'We will have a higher market share in our lead product than any of our competitors." You can then define an indicator to measure this statement as: "percentage of market share in lead product."

## Acceptance Criteria for Indicators

In order to be able to effectively measure your progress toward your vision, it is imperative that the indicators you design be of the highest possible quality. What does this mean? It means that they be measurable, supported by data, fact based, reliable, and accurately convey the intent of the vision. The descriptions below provide the characteristics the indicators should have:

➤ *Measurable.* The indicators should be measureable. An indicator is measurable if it begins with the words: number of, percent, ratio, average, sum, or delta (difference between A and B). Examples are: number of customer orders, percent of customer orders through online channels, average number of customer orders per day, total customer orders, difference between customer orders received versus projected.

➤ *Supported by data.* The indicator must be able to be supported by data that already exists in the company's data systems, or can be captured by examining the documents generated during the operation of the company processes. If data does not currently exist, you can assess whether data capture is possible or cost effective.

➤ *Fact-based.* Indicators are more meaningful if they are based on facts, not opinions. Although opinions may give valuable information, indicators based on facts are preferable. For example, an opinion-based indicator might be the percent of customers who rated the product with five stars on an ecommerce site. This is based on customer opinion. It is valuable information, but is not fact-based, whereas, the percentage of customers who ordered the product a second time is fact based. The more you make your indicator fact-based, the higher will be the quality of your measurement.

➤ *Reliable.* The data source you are considering for your indicator determines reliability. How reliable is the data accuracy from the source? How dependable is the source to provide the data on a regular basis?

➤ *Accurately conveys the intent of the vision.* If you have a choice of several indicators to measure the vision, the one that most accurately conveys the intent is the one you should choose. However, if data for this indicator does not exist or is difficult to obtain, then you can choose an indicator that closely approximates that intent.

Your company may currently be using metrics to track performance. How do these differ from the indicators of vision we are defining in this chapter? They don't. They are both indicators that measure progress. Your existing indicators are candidates to be linked to your vision. However, companies often have too many existing indicators and some might not be relevant and continue to be tracked from year to year. We suggest that you make a list of these indicators and analyze them one by one to see if they adequately describe the intent of any of the phrases in the vision statement. If they do, then they become vision indicators. If they don't, you might not need them.

To summarize, engage your team in clarifying your vision, then measuring the intent of your vision with the highest quality indicators that might include some of your existing indicators. Once you have developed your strategy, pick the indicators you need to focus on in the next twelve months. In the *Apply It* section, we provide you with an instrument to capture this work.

## ➤ APPLY IT: CREATE YOUR VISION TREE ←

Let's apply the concepts covered in this chapter to your company. First, you should facilitate the consultation process as we discussed in the last chapter, using the code of conduct to assure the right environment for the exchange of ideas. Your team will need to examine the statement you have defined for your vision and identify the key phrases. Then, you will need to describe the intent of the vision just as the team did in our case study at the top of this chapter. Don't be surprised if there is animated conversation and differences of opinion regarding the meaning of the terms. That is natural and healthy. The exchange of ideas is valuable and the consultation will lead to consensus.

Once you have a good definition of the intent for each vision phrase, you will be ready to engage your team by asking, "What information will tell us that we have achieved our intent?" Or, "What will indicate that we are moving towards our vision?' The answer to these questions will enable you to define an indicator to measure your progress. You could have one or more indicators for each element of your vision. Be sure that your indicators satisfy the acceptance criteria we have listed above. It would be helpful if you have a list of all the existing metrics of your company available as you are going through this exercise. You may select some of them to be included in the measurement of vision.

To organize your team's thinking and to facilitate the alignment process, you will find a structure called a "vision tree" useful. It is simply a tree that you create with the main branches linked to the key phrases of your vision and the sub-branches showing the indicators that measure their intent. Let's take the example of the XCorp Group. The key phrases or elements of their vision are:

- Preferred company with global footprint
- Outstanding value for customers
- Operational effectiveness
- Leadership in technology
- Excellent treatment of employees
- Satisfactory return on investment
- Contribution to the community

In Figure 3.1 on page 33 you will see these elements attached to the left side of the statements of mission and vision. These elements constitute the main branches of the tree.

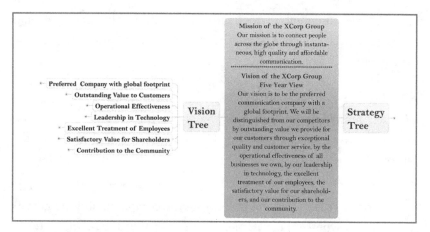

FIGURE 3.1 **The Main Branch of Vision Tree**

Now, look at each vision element and use the definition your team has provided on the intent of that element to see if one indicator could measure it or if you need several indicators. You may even need to break some indicators down further. Let's look at the XCorp example and see how the participants defined indicators for measuring the intent of their vision elements.

**Preferred Company with Global Footprint**

This implies being represented in major countries in the world and attracting customers through quality, service, or price. The indicators they picked for this vision element were:

➤ Top of mind to indicate the image of the company for attracting customers.

➤ Percent of market share of lead products and percent market share of strategic products to indicate how successful they are in taking customers away from competitors.

➤ Number of countries covered by the Group and number of countries in the number-one position to indicate the extent of their global footprint.

➤ Total worldwide sales and sales growth to indicate their increasing size consistent with their global footprint.

The measurement of their ability to attract customers through quality, service, or price would be covered under "outstanding value to customers."

## Outstanding Value to Customers

Value is related to the price customers pay for the goods or services as well as the quality of service. The indicators they defined for this vision element were:

➤ Percent growth in repeat sales to indicate the value the customers see by buying more from the company, and the growth of this percentage implies increasing the degree of customer satisfaction.

➤ Customer retention index is a similar measure. High scores for this index imply that you are not losing your customer base.

➤ Customer satisfaction index in quality measures the quality perceived by the customer through a customer survey.

➤ Customer satisfaction index in service could come from the same survey related to how the service was perceived by customers.

## Operational Effectiveness

The processes that deliver the value proposition to customers were different in the different businesses of XCorp. To measure this vision element, each business unit would have to compare its process effectiveness against best practice benchmarks. So, the indicators became:

➤ Percent compliance with benchmarks in sales
➤ Percent compliance with benchmarks in production
➤ Percent compliance with benchmarks in distribution
➤ Percent compliance with benchmarks in after sale customer support

## Leadership in Technology

To measure the intent of the XCorp Group to be the first to introduce the latest technology in its internal processes and in the products and services, they picked these indicators:

➤ Number of new breakthrough products to indicate how they had used technology to introduce successful new products.

➤ Number of months from design to market to show how quickly they were able to introduce new products to the customers. This was a critical factor in being first to make new technology available to customers.

➤ Percentage of sales from breakthrough technology to indicate how technology was affecting sales growth.

## Excellent Treatment of Employees

The consequence of good employee treatment is employee retention. The indicators they picked to measure this element were:

➤ Number of qualified applicants for a vacant position within the Group assuming that more qualified applicants meant more people were interested to work for XCorp.

➤ Percentage of reduction in undesirable turnover to indicate employees not leaving.

➤ Climate survey index to measure employee satisfaction.

## Satisfactory Value for Shareholders

Customer satisfaction will naturally result in shareholder satisfaction, which they measured by the following indicators:

➤ Economic Value Added (EVA) to measure the after tax profits less the cost of capital. This is a good indicator to illustrate how a business is accumulating value.

➤ Market Value Added (MVA) to indicate the effective market value measured by the difference between the market value of the company and the capital contributed by investors (both bondholders and shareholders).

➤ Earnings per share (EPS) to indicate the portion of a company's profit that is allocated to each outstanding share of common stock.

➤ EBITDA (Earnings before interest, taxes, depreciation and amortization) to show the company earnings.

**Contribution to the Community**

To measure XCorp's concern for the community, they picked the following indicators:

➤ Group corporate social responsibility (CSR) score to measure actions that appear to further some social good, beyond the interests of the firm and that which is required by law. This is an accepted index used by socially responsible companies.

➤ Contribution to worthy causes as percentage of sales to indicate the company's action in contributing to society.

➤ Recycled waste as percentage of total waste to measure the extent of recycling of waste materials used by the company.

The XCorp vision tree that includes these indicators is shown in Figure 3.2 on page 37. They were already tracking several of these indicators in some of the businesses. They decided to measure them across all business units. Your vision tree would look similar to this one.

The value add of this vision tree is that you will have a clear view of how your mission and vision are linked to specific measurement. You will be able to track your progress on these indicators.

Your aim is to construct a vision tree similar to Figure 3.2 on page 37 for your company. We provide a downloadable list of indicators in our website, www.totalalignment.com/pi, which can serve as a guide or a stimulus for your thinking. This list can help you in constructing your vision tree.

## ➤ THE NEXT STEPS ◄

The power of unity and clarity that comes from completing the vision tree is truly amazing, and we have seen it bear positive results with our clients. You will see how it will set into motion creative energies of your team and your organization toward achieving your vision. Your desire to reach your vision will translate into a creative strategy, which is the subject of the next chapter.

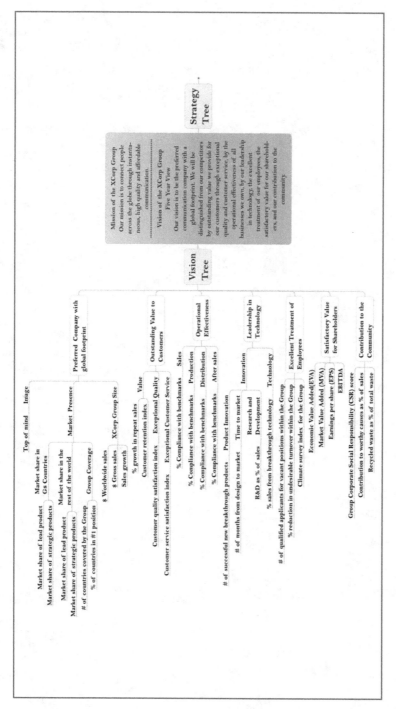

FIGURE 3.2  **XCorp Vision Tree**

# CHAPTER 4

# Aligning Strategy

The XCorp executives gather to see how the strategies of the businesses within the Group can become aligned and enable XCorp to progress towards its shared vision. In this chapter you will learn how you can use the XCorp strategic alignment example and align your strategy to deliver your own vision.

───────────────→ **THE CASE STUDY** ←───────────────

ONE MONTH LATER, Brian gathered the top teams of the XCorp Group for an offsite to discuss the strategy for the group of companies. The four CEOs of the business units (XCorpUS, IES, Cellular, and TechCorp) were present as well as four staff executives. Brian was mindful of the audacious vision they had come up with. His main concern now was how to achieve it. What gave him confidence was the fact that they had very strong investors who were providing solid financial backing. He felt that with the right focus and strategy, the group had a good chance of achieving their vision in the five-year period. He knew that one challenge he would face was the fact that each business unit head had his own ideas and goals and was focused mainly on expanding his own business. The key was to leverage the strength of each business and create synergy so that they could all work together to achieve a more shared vision.

After welcoming them to the meeting, Brian explained that the agenda for this offsite session was to talk about three components of strategy for the group:

➤ *Strategy for aligning the businesses*. While each business unit is autonomous and can determine its own strategy, its strategy should still be aligned with the group at large. One of the purposes of the offsite was to create guidelines for the business units in two categories: strategic direction and synergy mandate.

  – *Strategic direction*. This is the direction the businesses would follow related to aggressive growth or selective growth in segments or niches. As these growth options would require investment by the group, the direction would come from the group. It would be based on the relative strength of each business and the attractiveness of their market.

  – *Synergy mandate*. This is the collaboration and joining forces of the businesses within the group to create more value together than they would create individually.

➤ *Strategy for supporting the businesses*. This is a strategy to determine which processes common to all the businesses could be done more economically at the group level.

➤ *Strategy for acquiring new businesses*. When you develop an audacious vision, natural growth might not be enough to enable you to reach it. Part of the vision will need to be achieved through acquiring companies that fit within the group and add value.

Utilizing the data and information the business had prepared, the group came up with an initial draft of the Group Strategy.

## ──➤ ALIGN IT: ALIGNING VARIOUS BUSINESS ◄── STRATEGIES

In the case study you just read, the XCorp Group was searching for the right strategy to achieve its vision. The strategy pursued by each of their business units had contributed to the group's success, but then their vision became more audacious, the market forces were changing, and they needed to have a fresh look. Your company could be in a similar condition of being successful now, but requiring a creative strategy to move forward. While you will learn some ideas to assist you, we are not giving you a formula for determining your business strategy. You know your market, and strategy experts in your market can help you on your path to an excellent strategy.

What we are providing is mainly a way to align strategy, not create strategy. In this chapter, the XCorp Group is aligning the strategy of its current and future business units. They identified three key areas to examine: aligning the strategies of the businesses; supporting the businesses; and acquiring new businesses.

## *Aligning the Strategies of the Businesses*

In order to align the strategies of the businesses, the group examined two approaches: strategic direction and synergy mandate. Let's dig a little deeper into what those terms mean and talk about how they might work in a real-world context.

### Strategic Direction

By strategic direction, we mean the direction each business would need to follow in order to be aligned with the group. In the case study, the analysis the group decided to use was the modified GE-McKinsey Matrix, an excellent tool that has been used for years by many companies. Data had been prepared to support the analysis by the Planning Department. The result of the analysis was the position of each business on a two-dimensional grid, with the vertical axis showing the competitive position of the business relative to its strongest competitor and the horizontal axis showing its market attractiveness. Figure 4.1 on page 42 shows the position of each of the four businesses from our case study.

The grid shows XCorp US being much stronger than its closest competitor with its market being highly attractive as shown in Figure 4.1. Next ranked IES as somewhat stronger than its closest competitor and in an attractive market, but slightly less attractive than XCorp US. TechCorp and Cellular business were both evaluated as equal to their competitors, with TechCorp being in an extremely high-attractive market and Cellular in a medium-attractive market. Naturally, those businesses with high competitive positions and high market attractiveness would have the green light for aggressive growth while those with lower competitive positions and lower market attractiveness

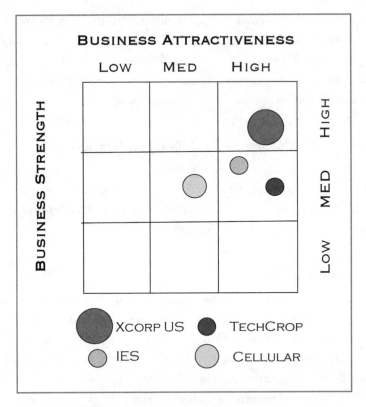

FIGURE 4.1 **XCorp Portfolio Analysis Grid**

would have to be more cautious. The size of the circle in the grid was an indicator of the relative size of the company in sales.

This analysis, along with the market knowledge that each participant brought, enabled the group to determine which business would have the group's financial support to grow aggressively, to grow selectively in niches, or to grow at all. The decision was based on the analysis of the position of each business on the grid as well as the sales and profitability of the business. This type of analysis led to the following "strategic direction" for the four businesses within the XCorp Group.

### Strategic Direction for the Businesses

➤ XCorp US will invest for aggressive growth and will seek dominance in the market.

➤ IES will invest strongly to grow market share in growth segments (to be identified).

➤ The Cellular business will invest to grow in selected segments of the market (to be identified).

➤ TechCorp will invest for aggressive growth worldwide and achieve a leadership position in selected market segments (to be identified).

With these types of statements as a guide, each business CEO can work with his team after the offsite to develop their core strategies. The exercise above is very valuable when a group has several business units, because the relative position of the portfolio of businesses can be seen visually on a grid and the decision about which ones to grow and which ones to divest becomes easier to make.

In the case of a company that has just one business unit, this exercise will also add value because it enables you to see your position on the grid and decide what direction to take. Obviously, if you are in a low-attractive market and weaker than your competitors, you would be very careful about investing to grow.

**Synergy Mandate**

In the story, having invested heavily in each business, the XCorp Group expects to benefit by synergies and can therefore demand it. Synergy mandates cause the businesses to complement one another and serve customer needs, reduce costs, increase differentiation, or enhance competitive advantage. Without this mandate, individual businesses might not make an effort to collaborate on their own. A synergy mandate could include two or more businesses joining forces, leveraging their capabilities, and sharing activities in the value chain. The synergy mandate for XCorp would look like this:

### Synergy Mandate

➤ Integrated Electronic Systems (IES), TechCorp, and Cellular will jointly develop prototypes of the next generation of communication devices using patented technologies within the group and other technologies to be acquired and will present the plans for development and distribution.

➤ XCorp US will provide its vast worldwide distribution channel to enable TechCorp's aggressive expansion worldwide and will share resources to achieve cost reduction and expedite service delivery.

This synergy mandate along with the strategic direction we described above, sums up what the group is asking businesses to do. But, what about the role of the group itself? Is it only to provide strategic direction and synergy mandate to the businesses? No, it could do more.

## Strategy for Supporting the Businesses

The group should examine processes that are common to all the businesses and do them at the group level where they can be carried out more economically. An example is talent management, which includes the selection, placement, evaluation, promotion, compensation, and development of talent. Another example is information technology and its use in integrating applications to manage the business and automate the back office functions. Each business could develop its own, or the group could provide the process to everyone, depending on which option is more cost effective. For a smaller business, these support functions are covered within the same business by different functional departments.

Some of these processes are already established in the business units and only need to be improved. Others are either nonexistent or are not adequate to deliver the vision. To formulate the group's strategy for supporting the businesses, look at each element in your own vision tree, and ask yourself whether the processes that currently exist for this element are adequate. If so, then nothing needs to be done at the group level. If not, then the group has the opportunity to create a new process for that element if it is a common process that benefits all its businesses.

Again, let's consider our fictional group as an example. Suppose that the participants examined the elements of the vision they had placed on the vision tree. Most of the common processes they were looking for already existed in the businesses. Two elements took the center stage in their discussions: excellent treatment of employees and innovation. Here is an example of the support strategy that XCorp Group developed.

### XCorp Strategy for Supporting the Businesses

New processes needed in the following areas:

➤ Excellent treatment of employees
➤ Innovation

The first element, "excellent treatment of employees," presented a challenge for TechCorp, in particular. At TechCorp, highly technical talent, which had been developed in-house, suddenly decided to leave. The strategic initiatives for this area became:

➤ Develop and implement a plan to transfer best human resource practices to all businesses, to attract and retain talent.
➤ Plan and implement processes to spread the group values of excellence across businesses.

The second element, "innovation," was a topic all the businesses were keenly interested in. This element is definitely important to everyone. After further consultation they decided that many innovative ideas naturally emerge in the field in response to customer needs. When a customer has a need not covered by existing products or services, and the company responds by developing a feature or a new capability that meets that need, the new capability can become the desired innovation, provided that it also satisfies the needs of hundreds and even thousands of customers. The strategic initiative for this area became: Establish and fund an office to provide financial support to businesses in developing new products or services for their markets.

## *Strategy for Acquiring New Businesses*

When you develop an audacious vision, natural growth might not be enough to enable you to reach it. Assuming that you have access to capital, a good strategy might be to grow through acquisition. The initiatives necessary to determine the need for acquisitions and to acquire companies were:

- Establish criteria for determining size
- Analyze existing potential for natural growth
- Develop a plan to maximize synergies to increase sales
- Establish acquisition criteria and plan
- Execute existing planned acquisitions

While the businesses within the group can each pursue acquisitions that are appropriate for their own growth and receive the group's approval, the group itself must pursue a strategy for acquiring new businesses consistent with its mission and vision.

## ⟶ APPLY IT: BUILD YOUR STRATEGY TREE ◄—

If your company has multiple business units, then you are a Group by our definition and much of what we have described here will apply. In summary, you display your mission and vision on the screen for your team to view and also the grid of the position of each of the businesses. Together you decide which ones should receive the investment to grow aggressively, which ones to grow in niches, which ones to stay on a maintenance mode, and which ones to divest. You provide strategic direction to the businesses and allow them to develop their own strategy aligned with the direction. You also require the businesses to complement each other and collaborate to add greater value to the Group. The gap between what your existing businesses can accomplish through natural growth and what is required in your vision statement will be yours to fill through strategic acquisitions.

If you are a single business unit or a smaller startup, then you display your mission and vision for your team and determine where you are by calculating the status of the indicators of your vision tree. Next, you will need to plot your position on a grid with the vertical axis being business strength and the horizontal axis being market attractiveness. Based on where you are, a suitable direction will emerge. If you are in low strength and low attractiveness, then investment to grow your existing business will not be wise, and you might have to revisit your business concept, and modify or tone down your vision. If you are in the high strength and high attractiveness position, then aggressive growth would be an option. Look at your vision and if it is really ambitious, and your market is highly attractive, than at some point in the future you might need to consider acquisition.

To organize your thinking around aligning strategy, we want to introduce you to a structure of a strategy tree that serves as an instrument of alignment. Like the vision tree, this instrument serves to capture the concepts of this chapter and provides a framework for sustaining alignment. Figure 4.2 on page 48 is an example of the strategy tree for the XCorp Group. The three main branches of this tree, as explained above, are Strategy for Aligning the Businesses, Strategy for Supporting the Businesses, and Strategy for Acquiring New Businesses.

### *Strategy for Aligning Businesses*

This tree will have several sub-branches and sub-sub-branches ending up with clear actions your team (or teams) can perform, or strategic initiatives they can implement. When you have transferred your alignment concepts onto this tree, you will have a set of important strategic actions to pursue and a set of important strategic initiatives to implement.

Let's put the sub-branches on the XCorp strategy tree associated with the first main branch, "Strategy for Aligning the Businesses." The two sub-branches would be "Strategic Direction for the Portfolio of Businesses" owned by the Group and "Synergy Mandate" as shown in Figure 4.3 on page 48.

FIGURE 4.2 **XCorp Strategy Tree—Main Branches**

Adding the strategic direction for the portfolio of businesses would produce the expanded sub-branches as seen in Figure 4.4 on page 49.

The strategic direction for the XCorp US for example says, "Invest for aggressive growth and seek to dominate the market." How does XCorp US do that? Where is its strategy? The right-

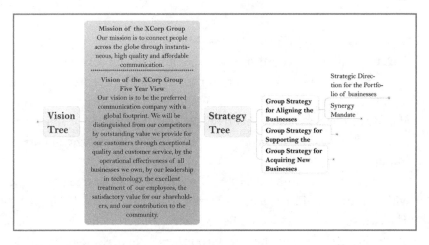

FIGURE 4.3 **XCorp Strategy Tree—Sub-Branches**

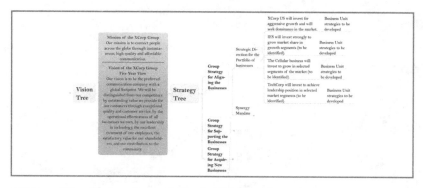

FIGURE 4.4  **XCorp Strategy Tree—Expanded Sub-Branch**

most sub-branch in Figure 4.4 says, "Business unit strategies to be developed." Well, we can assume that the XCorp US CEO would go back and assemble his executive team along with industry experts and figure that out. Naturally, they would use well-known analytical tools such as the popular SWOT analysis (strengths, weaknesses, opportunities, and threats) to read their reality. This analysis basically requires them to list the areas where their business is strong or weak as compared to competitors, the opportunities ahead, and the threats to the business. The information can then help them devise appropriate strategies to leverage their strengths and overcome their weaknesses and to develop initiatives to explore the attractive opportunities. Additionally, they would perform an in-depth forecast of market trends, competitive forces, and consider recent concepts, such as platforms. Based on such analysis and solid data, they would arrive at the right strategy for the strategic direction mandated by the Group. Adding the synergy mandate to the strategy tree will complete the Group strategy for aligning the businesses as shown in Figure 4.5 on page 50. The quality of the strategy that emerges will be key to the survival and success of the company for years to come.

### *Strategy for Supporting Businesses*

While the work of completing the sub-branches for the main branch, "Strategy for Aligning the Businesses" is left to be

**Vision Tree**

Mission of the XCorp Group
Our mission is to connect people across the globe through instantaneous, high quality and affordable communication.

Vision of the XCorp Group
Five Year View
Our vision is to be the preferred communication company with a global footprint. We will be distinguished from our competitors by outstanding value we provide for our customers through exceptional quality and customer service, by the operational effectiveness of all businesses we own, by our leadership in technology, the excellent treatment of our employees, the satisfactory value for our shareholders, and our contribution to the community.

**Strategy Tree**

**Group Strategy for Aligning the Businesses**

Strategic Direction for the Portfolio of businesses

XCorp US will invest for aggressive growth and will seek dominance in the market.

IES will invest strongly to grow market share in growth segments (to be identified).

The Cellular business will invest to grow in selected segments of the market (to be identified).

TechCorp will invest to achieve leadership position in selected market segments (to be identified).

Business Unit strategies to be developed

Business Unit strategies to be developed

Business Unit strategies to be developed

Business Unit strategies to be developed

**Synergy Mandate**

Integrated Electronic Systems (IES), TechCorp and Cellular will jointly develop prototypes of the next generation of communication devices using patented technologies within the Group and other technologies to be acquired, and will present the plans for development and distribution.

Xcorp and TechCorp will share resources to achieve cost reduction and expedite service delivery.

Synergy strategies to be developed

Synergy strategies to be developed

**Group Strategy for Supporting the Businesses**

**Group Strategy for Acquiring New Businesses**

FIGURE 4.5  XCorp Strategy Tree—All Branches for Aligning the Businesses

completed within the business units, the ideas for the second main branch, "Strategy for Supporting the Businesses" is developed by the Group itself and can be added to the strategy tree. Take a look at Figure 4.6 on page 52 to see how that translates for our XCorp example.

### *Strategy for Acquiring New Businesses*

When we add the initiatives related to acquiring new businesses, we will have the full strategy tree for your company similar to the setup in Figure 4.7 on page 53.

### *Strategic Actions and Strategic Initiatives*

The fruits of the strategy tree are strategic actions and strategic initiatives. Strategic actions are single actions to be completed with quality by a certain future deadline. Strategic initiatives are strategic projects that include project plans, milestones, and multiple actions to be completed by a certain future deadline. Examples of strategic actions are: "Obtain a permit for construction by June 1," or "Present a list of potential candidates by September 1." Both of these examples are single actions to be accomplished by a deadline. An example of an initiative might be something like: "Construct a plant X to boost our production capacity by 50 percent." This is an initiative with multiple actions following a project plan with milestones and deliverables. You should be sure that actions and strategic initiatives are stated in a clear manner, each one stating a tangible deliverable.

## ➤ THE NEXT STEPS ◄

We have introduced the concepts involved in creating the vision tree and the strategy tree. Now we are ready to put them together. In the next chapter, you will see how these two trees join to become an important framework for aligning the organization.

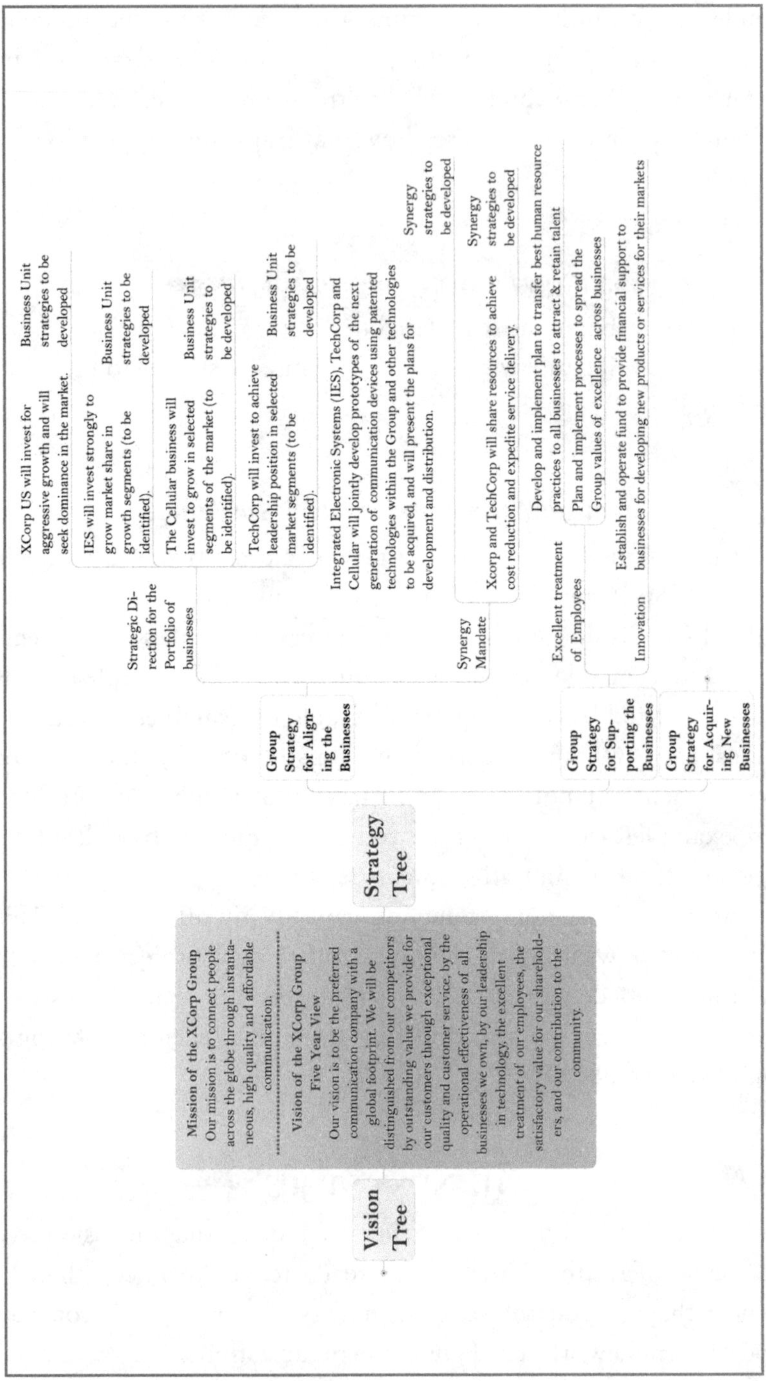

FIGURE 4.6   XCorp Strategy Tree—Strategy for Supporting the Businesses

**Strategic Direction for the Portfolio of businesses**

XCorp US will invest for aggressive growth and will seek dominance in the market.

IES will invest strongly to grow market share in growth segments (to be identified).

The Cellular business will invest to grow in selected segments of the market (to be identified).

TechCorp will invest to achieve leadership position in selected market segments (to be identified).

Business Unit strategies to be developed

Business Unit strategies to be developed

Business Unit strategies to be developed

**Synergy Mandate**

Integrated Electronic Systems (IES), TechCorp and Cellular will jointly develop prototypes of the next generation of communication devices using patented technologies within the Group and other technologies to be acquired, and will present the plans for development and distribution.

Xcorp and TechCorp will share resources to achieve cost reduction and expedite service delivery.

Synergy strategies to be developed

Synergy strategies to be developed

**Group Strategy for Aligning the Businesses**

**Excellent treatment of Employees**

Develop and implement plan to transfer best human resource practices to all businesses to attract & retain talent

Plan and implement processes to spread the Group values of excellence across businesses

**Innovation**

Establish and operate fund to provide financial support to businesses for developing new products or services for their markets

**Group Strategy for Supporting the Businesses**

**Xcorp Group Size**

Establish criteria for determining size, propose strategy for increasing size and coordinate with business units to implement

**Group Strategy natural Growth**

Analyze existing potential for natural growth, propose growth segments, and coordinate with businesses to consult about implementation

Develop & implement plan to maximize synergies to increase sales

**Group Strategy acquisitions**

Execute existing planned acquisition in collaboration with finance and business leaders

Establish acquisition criteria, develop plan and implement plan after approval by XCorp Group

**Group Coverage**

Develop and implement a plan to maximize coverage worldwide

**Group Strategy for Acquiring New Businesses**

**Strategy Tree**

**Mission of the XCorp Group**
Our mission is to connect people across the globe through instantaneous, high quality and affordable communication.

**Vision of the XCorp Group Five Year View**
Our vision is to be the preferred communication company with a global footprint. We will be distinguished from our competitors by outstanding value we provide for our customers through exceptional quality and customer service, by the operational effectiveness of all businesses we own, by our leadership in technology, the excellent treatment of our employees, the satisfactory value for our shareholders, and our contribution to the community.

**Vision Tree**

FIGURE 4.7  XCorp Full Strategy Tree

**CHAPTER 5**

# The Alignment Map

The XCorp executives are now ready to think strategically about their next step in alignment—the Alignment Map. You will learn how to combine the vision tree and the strategy tree to build your own alignment map, which is your roadmap for success.

## ➤ THE CASE STUDY ◄

WHEN THE XCORP executives gathered the next morning, they saw their Alignment Map projected on a screen. They recognized the vision tree on the left side and the strategy tree on the right. This map illustrated what it would take for the vision of XCorp Group to be realized. Mark, the "Infoman," explained that the map would become the key to aligning the organization and would serve as a frame of reference for every action. As the alignment map is so important to the future of the company, they would have to assure its high quality.

They spent time consulting together and reviewing each side of the map (Figure 5.1 on page 56). They discussed how the implementation of the strategic initiatives listed on the right side would, in time, impact the indicators on the left side, and consequently advance them toward their vision.

**Strategy Tree**

**Vision Tree**

Mission of the XCorp Group
Our mission is to connect people across the globe through instantaneous, high quality and affordable communication.

Vision of the XCorp Group
Five Year View
Our vision is to be the preferred communication company with a global footprint. We will be distinguished from our competitors by outstanding value we provide for our customers through exceptional quality and customer service, by the operational effectiveness of all businesses we own, by our leadership in technology, the excellent treatment of our employees, the satisfactory value for our shareholders, and our contribution to the community.

**Strategy Tree**

Strategic Direction for the Portfolio of businesses
- XCorp US will invest for aggressive growth and will seek dominance in the market. → Business Unit strategies to be developed
- IES will invest strongly to grow market share in growth segments (to be identified). → Business Unit strategies to be developed
- The Cellular business will invest to grow in selected segments of the market (to be identified). → Business Unit strategies to be developed
- TechCorp will invest to achieve leadership position in selected market segments (to be identified). → Business Unit strategies to be developed

Group Strategy for Aligning the Businesses

Synergy Mandate
- Integrated Electronic Systems (IES), TechCorp and Cellular will jointly develop prototypes of the next generation of communication devices using patented technologies within the Group and other technologies to be acquired, and will present the plans for development and distribution. → Synergy strategies to be developed
- Xcorp and TechCorp will share resources to achieve cost reduction and expedite service delivery. → Synergy strategies to be developed

Group Strategy for Supporting the Businesses

Excellent treatment of Employees
- Develop and implement plan to transfer best human resource practices to all businesses to attract & retain talent
- Plan and implement processes to spread the Group values of excellence across businesses

Innovation
- Establish and operate fund to provide financial support to businesses for developing new products or services for their markets

Group Strategy for Acquiring New Businesses

Xcorp Group Size

Group Strategy natural Growth
- Establish criteria for determining size, propose strategy for increasing size and coordinate with business units to implement
- Analyze existing potential for natural growth, propose growth segments, and coordinate with businesses to consult about implementation
- Develop & implement plan to maximize synergies to increase sales

Group Strategy acquisitions
- Execute existing planned acquisition in collaboration with finance and business leaders
- Establish acquisition criteria, develop plan and implement plan after approval by XCorp Group

Group Coverage
- Develop and implement a plan to maximize coverage worldwide

**Vision Tree**

Preferred Company with global footprint

Market Presence
- Top of mind
- Image
- Market share in Cis Countries
- Market share in the rest of the world
- Market share of lead product
- Market share of strategic products
- Market share of lead product
- Market share of strategic products

Group Coverage
- # of countries covered by the Group
- % of countries in #1 position

XCorp Group Size
- $ Worldwide sales
- $ Gross sales
- Sales growth
- % growth in repeat sales

Outstanding Value to Customers

Value
- Customer retention index

Exceptional Quality
- Customer quality satisfaction index

Exceptional Customer Service
- Customer service satisfaction index

Operational Effectiveness
- Sales — % Compliance with benchmarks
- Production — % Compliance with benchmarks
- Distribution — % Compliance with benchmarks
- After sales

Leadership in Technology

Product Innovation
- # of successful new breakthrough products
- # of months from design to market

Innovation
- Time to market
- Research and Development

Technology
- % sales from breakthrough technology

Excellent Treatment of Employees
- # of qualified applicants for vacant positions within the Group
- % reduction in undesirable turnover within the Group
- Climate survey index for the Group

Satisfactory Value for Shareholders
- Economic Value Added(EVA)
- Market Value Added (MVA)
- Earnings per share (EPS)
- EBITDA

Contribution to the Community
- Group Corporate Social Responsibility (CSR) score
- Contribution to worthy causes as % of sales
- Recycled waste as % of total waste

FIGURE 5.1  The Alignment Map for XCorp Group

The participants spent the rest of their morning session discussing how they could improve the quality of the map.

# ➤ ALIGN IT: MEASURING STRATEGIC ← INITIATIVES

There is a fundamental need for a tangible frame of reference that can be used for aligning organizations. This is where the Alignment Map comes into play. We developed the Alignment Map to serve as a compass and a guide for the alignment process. Its goal is to focus everyone on those key factors that will lead to success.

Now, let's take a look at both sides of the Map. Both sides should have measurable indicators. The left side has the indicators of vision that were discussed in Chapter 3. The right side has a list of strategic actions and strategic initiatives as discussed in Chapter 4. You will learn in this chapter that these are also measurable, and you will see a methodology for measuring them.

## *Measurement for the Right Side*

An initiative is a project. In the case of alignment, we use the word "initiative" to describe a strategic project of high importance rather than ordinary, everyday projects that companies have in place. The real measurement of the success of a project is the result it produces. The result is fact-based, but unfortunately only available after the project is completed. What about measurement of the project before completion? One alternative is to measure the progress of the project against a set of criteria. Such measurement will be partially based on opinion, but still valuable. It can provide an early warning when the project is not doing well and will allow for intervention and course adjustment.

Let's start by defining what makes a project, an initiative, successful. A project is successful if it has the elements of success before, during, and after implementation. Here are the characteristics you need before implementation of a successful initiative:

- ➤ Good project plan with the right milestones and deliverables
- ➤ Clear objectives for the project to deliver after implementation
- ➤ Customer involvement to define the quality specifications and delivery date
- ➤ Allocated funds to assure the project can pay for the resources it needs
- ➤ Assignment of the right resources
- ➤ Committed and competent person in charge as a project manager

When these characteristics are present, the project has an excellent chance of tangible success. However, most projects will encounter challenges during execution that could not have been foreseen and the project plan will need to be dynamically adjusted. Here are the characteristics you need during implementation of an initiative:

- ➤ Update of the schedule based on a revised project plan
- ➤ Quality of work based on the customer specifications provided before starting
- ➤ Customer involvement during the implementation to assure satisfaction
- ➤ On-time delivery of the project milestones
- ➤ On budget in terms of use of resources to reach the milestones
- ➤ Good project management

Paying attention to these characteristics will increase the chances of project success. If any of these characteristics is absent, the project manager will need to determine the causes for the missing item and find the remedy. Here are some characteristics for a successful project after execution:

- ➤ The objectives of the project are met and the benefits are measurable
- ➤ The project outcome meets or exceeds the expected quality
- ➤ The customers are satisfied
- ➤ The project is delivered on time
- ➤ The project is completed within budget
- ➤ The project has post delivery service

| Before Implementation | During Implementation | After Implementation |
|---|---|---|
| Good plan | Updated schedule | Benefits |
| Clear objectives | Quality of work | Quality of outcome |
| Customer involvement | Customer involvement | Customer satisfaction |
| Allocated funds | On-time on milestones | On-time delivery |
| Assigned resources | On budget on milestones | On budget on delivery |
| Committed person in charge | Good project management | Post delivery service |

FIGURE 5.2 **Requirements for Excellent Execution**

These characteristics are summarized in a chart in Figure 5.2. When all the characteristics are fulfilled, then the project has excellent execution.

Assuming that the criteria for starting the project are met, the measurement of progress will be based on the items in the middle column of Figure 5.2. Evaluation based on these criteria will be necessary on a regular basis. Who should do the evaluating? Select one or more individuals within your organization or external people who would benefit most from the project and would agree to act as its customers. The customers of the initiative will rate its progress monthly using any combination of the characteristics listed.

When there are multiple customers of an initiative, their evaluation should be combined with some weighting criteria based on the value of the project to their areas. For example, if there are three customers, you could assign the weight of 20, 30, and 50 to them respectively. Calculate a weighted average of the evaluations from these customers. When this number is low, the person accountable for the initiative will have to analyze all the evaluations and determine a plan of action to bring the project into compliance.

We call the index that measures the progress of the initiative in this manner an INX, which stands for INitiative indeX. The right side of the alignment map will have INXs associated with the strategic initiatives. As the number associated with INX is based on opinions of the key customers, it is not as a precise measurement of progress, but an indicator to alert when the initiative has problems. Nevertheless, to make the evaluations as objective as possible, the on-time advance of the project should be based on its meeting milestone in a project plan, rather than the opinion of the customer.

### *Focusing on the Vital Few*

Our experience shows that often companies attempt to implement too many initiatives beyond their ability to execute them well. It is important to prioritize. Here are a few tips for prioritizing the initiatives to focus on:

- *Use the Pareto principle.* Twenty percent of what you do will have eighty percent of the impact. As the Pareto principle is fractal, twenty percent of the twenty percent is truly significant, and only a vital few can add tremendous value. To determine the vital few, look at the list of your initiatives on the right side of your alignment map and pick the top set of initiatives that will deliver 80 percent impact on your vision. Focus on those initiatives.
- *Use the Cause and Effect principle.* Each strategic initiative will have an impact on the indicators you have already defined for the vision tree. Some will impact multiple indicators of high importance. By analyzing the cause and effect relationship of the strategic initiatives with the key indicators, you will be able to eliminate those that are less important.
- *Use the weighting concept.* As your financial and human resources are limited, you will not be able to do all the initiatives you have identified. So pick the most important ones. To do this, you can distribute 100 points among the initiatives and pick those with the highest weights.
- *Use the sequencing concept.* The large list of initiatives you have developed is intended to help you achieve the vision of the

company. Usually, your vision expands over many years, and therefore not all the initiatives need to start immediately. By sequencing those that should be done this year versus those that can wait, you will be able to reduce your list to the vital few.

## ➤ APPLY IT: CONSTRUCT YOUR ALIGNMENT MAP ◂

If you have followed the process we have described in the previous chapters, you already have the first version of your alignment map. To assure the quality of this map, we suggest that you first examine each side independently to improve quality as described below, then follow the validation check that considers both sides of the map and their mutual relationships.

### *Improving the Quality of the Left Side*

To be sure that the indicators meet the quality criteria mentioned in Chapter 3, that they are measureable, supported by data, fact-based, reliable, and adequately convey the intent of the vision, we suggest the following. Test your indicators by calculating the status. This will ensure that you have the right formula and data.

Some of your indicators will have no data and you will not be able to calculate current status. What would you do in that situation? Here are a couple of suggestions. If the indicator is related to existing processes try to change the way you have defined the indicator and use the data that you have available. For example, you might not have data on "employee satisfaction index," but could have data on "organizational climate survey." Use the data you have and estimate the cost of new data capture versus the benefit of retaining the indicator. This will help you decide to keep your indicator, replace it with another, or delete it.

Regarding the ones that are not relevant now because the processes don't yet exist, leave them on the map so the numbers can be calculated in the future. Be sure your indicators adequately measure the intent of the vision and are strategic indicators. In other words, that they support the implementation of strategy. And, finally, make sure they are prioritized with a focus on the few significant indicators.

### *Improving the Quality of the Right Side*

The quality of the right side of your alignment map is primarily determined by the quality of the business strategy you have developed. Take the time to ascertain that the right strategy for competition and growth is developed for the business. Include the following criteria:

➤ The strategy is converted into the right initiatives
➤ You are focusing on the vital few
➤ The initiatives are assigned to the right project manager
➤ Customers are assigned to each initiative

Ask the customers to evaluate the initiative using the appropriate criteria. Figure 5.3 on page 63 gives you a sample questionnaire that can be used by the customers.

To improve the quality of the information that supports the INX evaluation, you will need to reduce the subjectivity of the evaluation. Here are a few ideas that could help you do that:

➤ The evaluation by customers should be based on solid data coming from a good project management tool that tracks project steps, milestones, deliverables, and critical path. You need to use a project management tool.
➤ Insist that project plans show documented updates from month to month.
➤ Insist that quality specifications are in place to help the customer of the initiative in the evaluation process.
➤ Insist that the customers who evaluate the on-time and on-budget criteria use data to support their assessment.
➤ Have two or more customers evaluate the initiative.

In summary, you have now created a guide for your organization to become aligned. Refer to this map often in the gatherings of your executives. Use the mission and vision statement at its center to

| Strategic Initiative: | Project Manager: | | Customer: | | Date: | |
|---|---|---|---|---|---|---|
| Criteria | Weight | Rating | Back Up Source | Weighted Score | Comments | |
| The initiative has an updated project plan with milestones and deliverables | 10 | Yes or no | Project plan | | | |
| The initiative progress on milestones is on time | 30 | Yes or no | Project plan | | | |
| The initiative is within the allocated budget | 20 | Yes or no | Project expense | | | |
| The initiative milestone meets the quality specification | 20 | Yes or no | Quality document | | | |
| The customers of the initiative are satisfied with the progress | 20 | Yes or no | Customer view | | | |
| | | | Total | | | |

FIGURE 5.3  Strategic Initiative Progress Evaluation

remind everyone of the inspiring mission you have fashioned and the audacious goal ahead. Use the left side to evaluate how your company is progressing towards its goals and the right side to remind everyone of the key strategies in place, their progress, and how they are contributing to your advancement.

——————————➤ THE NEXT STEPS ◄——————————

Now, you can assign individual accountability for the indicators and strategic initiatives you have identified. We will discuss how to do that in the next chapter.

# CHAPTER 6

# Accountability

The Alignment Map that emerged from the gathering of the XCorp executives provided a great deal of clarity for everyone present. They could see how the indicators and initiatives in measureable form help the company advance towards its vision. The next step in the process is to figure out who is accountable for each indicator and initiative. You will learn how to apply the XCorp example to define accountability in your organization.

## THE CASE STUDY

THE INFOMAN introduced some concepts to the group that would allow accountability to be assigned effectively. The process indicators (located on the left side of the map) would be assigned to the person at the lowest appropriate level of the organization who has the most direct impact on improving the indicator. The initiative indicators (located on the right side of the map) would be assigned to the person at the highest appropriate level of the organization with the most direct impact on the success of the initiative.

He went on to explain the rationale behind these guidelines. Processes are well defined in the organization and people who manage those processes should be held accountable for the indicator. These people are usually at the lower levels of the organization. But strategic initiatives involve creating something new and require a budget. A person with a greater scope of authority who is at a higher level in the organization would have the decision-making power and credibility to bring the right resources together to make the initiative successful.

Both process indicators and initiative indicators are influenced by several people, each person performing a different role. There are four clear roles: direct impact, cross-functional influence, management influence, and doted-line or matrix influence. The group reviewed each process indicator and initiative indicator on the Alignment Map and identified the people who would have the appropriate roles for each indicator. They documented the person and the role for each indicator and initiative. This way they were able to have a clear picture of accountability for every aspect of the Map.

## ────►ALIGN IT: CREATING A FRAMEWORK◄────
## FOR ACCOUNTABILITY

As the case study points out, all the measurements (indicators and initiatives) on the Alignment Map must be assigned to someone. On the left side of the map, where the process indicators are located, the accountability should be pushed down to the lowest appropriate level. This gives the power to act to the right person, thus empowering all levels of employees. In many organizations, decisions are made at the wrong level, sometimes several levels removed from the person whose action can impact the indicator. This not only creates confusion, but distracts your team (or teams) from meeting their individual goals.

The reverse is true for the right side of the map. The initiatives should be assigned to the highest appropriate level in the organization. The word "appropriate" implies that the person has the decision making power to allocate necessary resources to ensure the success of the initiative. Because of the high importance of strategic projects for the future of the business, the person in charge should be as close to the CEO level as possible. This could imply that all of these initiatives should be assigned to the CEO. However, one person will not have time to be the project manager for all strategic projects. Some projects can be assigned to a direct report of the CEO or another appropriate person.

## *The Four Roles in Accountability*

There are four roles that could be assigned to the indicators and initiatives. Defining these roles clarifies accountability and ensures that each person understands how their actions impact the indicator. Each person with indispensable influence on an indicator will have one of these four roles.

### The Role of Direct Influence or CSF

The person with the greatest direct impact on moving a process indicator, at the lowest level in the organization, is accountable for the indicator. The indicator becomes the person's critical success factor (CSF). The CSF takes the value of the indicator.

For example, if the indicator is "percent customer returns" and John is the person in charge of production at the lowest level of the organization with the greatest direct impact, then John's CSF is "percent customer returns." If the status of the indicator is 5 percent for a particular month, then the CSF of John will also have the value of 5 percent.

Let's take another example, "percent undesirable turnover of salespeople." This is an indicator that measures how fast you are losing your sales talent. The person with the most direct influence on this indicator is the sales manager. Therefore, this is his CSF. If the status of the indicator is 10 percent for a particular month, then the CSF will have the same value of 10 percent.

### The Role of Cross-Functional Influence or CIF

Rarely is there an indicator that is influenced by only one person. Usually, there are many people in different functional areas who influence the same indicator. To capture this shared responsibility, we define the role of cross-functional influence and assign a term called a critical influence factor (CIF) to those people who have indispensable cross-functional influence on a factor but are not the main drivers.

Consider the two examples above. In the first case, "customer returns" could be impacted by different functions, including the shipping supervisor, salesperson, and marketing supervisor. As such, each of these individuals will have "percent customer returns" as their CIF, and the status of their indicator will be the same as the status of the CSF, that is, 5 percent.

In the second example, "percent undesirable turnover of salespeople," could be influenced cross-functionally by the human resource manager, who will have the indicator as a CIF, with the same value of 10 percent as the owner of the CSF.

Think about your own company. Suppose you are a marketing manager. What would be one of your CSFs and one of your CIFs? One of your CSFs would be the interest you generate through your marketing efforts measured by the number of clicks on an online ad or the number of responses to a television commercial. Your CIF could be "$ sales" because your marketing efforts will produce more sales, so you have an indispensable influence. The indicator "$ sales" is a CSF for the salesperson and CIF for you. There are other jobs in the company that would have CIF for sales as well, such as the production manager or the logistics manager, because they both have an indispensable influence on sales.

When the roles of CSF and CIF are clarified, the owner of a CSF knows that the company expects results from her, and this is motivating. The owner of a CIF knows that he is expected to collaborate to influence the result. However, the CIF owner will also realize that it is important to not take over the role that the CSF owner must play. Through the process of involvement everyone understands their role and agrees with it. This increases collaboration.

### The Role of Management Influence or CMF

The third role is that of management influence. If you impact an indicator through your role as a manager, then the indicator will be a critical management factor (CMF) for you. A CMF measures your success at influencing results through the people you manage. For example, as a sales manager, the total sales of the six salespersons reporting to you would be your critical management factor. It is a

CMF because you don't do the actual selling, but you influence the sales through your salespeople.

If you are a manager, you will also have individual CSFs for your job. Beyond watching the total consolidated number as a CMF, you have a unique contribution to make that is measurable. For example, as a sales manager, one unique contribution and CSF for you could be "percent of your salespersons over quota." This encourages you to pay attention to all your salespeople and help them achieve their quota, and it contributes to a long-term development of your resources. Another CSF could be "percent of salespersons that achieve 120 percent of their quota." This encourages you to pay attention to the high-performing salespersons who work to increase the overall sales.

Distinguishing the CSFs from CMFs is very important, because the tendency in many organizations is for managers and directors to consider consolidated numbers from lower levels as their own CSFs. This causes layers in the organization "watching" those actually doing the work. For example, suppose you have five people selling. A zone manager would be looking at the total sales of the zone. The regional manager would be looking at the total sales for all the zones. The country manager would be looking the total sales of all the regions. That's fine and that is their CMF. But what other added value do they have? It is important to be able to identify unique added value for each job and assign CSFs to the job.

If you are a smaller company that doesn't have the complex structure of a large one, the concepts of CSF and CMF still apply as long as you have more than one level. You may have a few managers handling your sales, production, and delivery who each have people reporting to them. What we are suggesting is that the accountability for the indicators in your alignment map should be distributed among people with specific roles of CSF, CIF, and CMF that are well defined.

### The Role of Dotted Line Influence or CIM

The fourth role is the "dotted line" influence. This role is called CIM, which stands for critical influence management factor. It implies the management influence over the work of an individual in a different function (dotted line). To look at an example of a dotted line influence, let's imagine a large department store. In the men's department, there is a boutique line of sunglasses. The salespeople are selling a mix of products including the boutique line of sunglasses. The sales people report to the sales manager of their department in a solid line for the total sales in their areas. They could have a dotted line reporting to a director in the store responsible for the sunglass category. So the measurement "$ sales of sunglasses" would be a CSF for the salespeople, a CMF for the sales manager, and a CIM for the category director.

### Accountability Roles for Initiative Indicators

The roles we have described for the process indicators (left side of map) also apply to the initiative indicators on the right side of the Alignment Map. As we discussed in Chapter 5, the initiatives on the right side have indicators as well. You evaluate their progress through a basket of criteria mentioned in the last chapter.

As mentioned in the last chapter, an indicator on the right side of the map is called INX (or INitiative IndeX) because it is an index of the progress of an initiative. Similar to CSFs, the INXs come in four types. The ones that you have the greatest direct influence on are your Initiative Indexes or INXs. The initiatives that you influence through your role as a manager are your Initiative Management Indexes or IMXs. The initiatives that you have indispensable influence on through your cross-functional role are your Initiative Influence Indexes or INIs. And the initiatives that you influence through your dotted line management role are your Initiative Management Influence Indexes or IMIs.

Let's look at a few examples of initiative indicators. Suppose your company has a strategy of implementing a new module to automate your back office functions, and you assign one person in each department to oversee the project. You would assign accountability as INX to the project managers within each department for implementing this initiative, and the person who oversees the implementation for the whole company would have the role of IMX.

Here is another example. Suppose you are a small company in the restaurant business and want to expand from your home base to three restaurants in three cities. Opening the restaurant would be an INX for three individuals, one for each city. The key managers in your home restaurant could have a role of INI, and you could assign one person overseeing all three projects whose role would be IMX consolidating the progress of the three restaurants.

### *Summary of Roles in Accountability*

The summary of the concepts just described is presented in Figure 6.1. You can use it as a reference when assigning accountability for indicators from your Alignment Map.

Let's summarize the main points in this chapter. The Alignment Map has two types of indicators, those that are linked to vision and those that are linked to strategy. The indicators linked to vision from the left side of the map are assigned to the individual at the lowest appropriate level of the organization as a critical success factor, or CSF. The indicators from the right side of the map, dealing with strategy, are assigned to the highest appropriate level

| Type of Impact | Impact on Vision Indicators | Impact on Strategic Initiatives |
|---|---|---|
| Direct Impact | Critical Success Factor (CSF) | Initiative Index (INX) |
| Management Influence | Critical Management Factor (CMF) | Initiative Management Index (IMX) |
| Cross-Functional Influence | Critical Influence Factor (CIF) | Initiative Influence Index (INI) |
| Cross-Functional Dotted Line Management Influence | Critical Influence Management Factor (CIM) | Initiative Management Influence Index (IMI) |

FIGURE 6.1 **Accountability Concepts**

in the organization as an INX. Besides the person who has the prime responsibility, other individuals assume roles of indispensable influence. Figure 6.1 summarizes these roles.

## ➤ APPLY IT: ASSIGN ACCOUNTABILITY FACTORS ◄
## TO YOUR TEAM

Let's apply the accountability process to your organization. You need to invite the appropriate people to the meeting for assigning accountability. The facilitation of this accountability process is critical to the right definition. Have a skilled facilitator guide the process using the "Code of Conduct" we described in previous chapters to encourage everyone to contribute to a meaningful conversation. Who should be included in the conversation? The top team of the company as well as representatives from the jobs should be invited. If you have twenty people doing the same job, you could invite one or two representatives from the job. If you are a small company, you can invite all your managers to the conversation.

Because you have already created your Alignment Map, assigning the factors to the right people is not difficult if you follow this methodology:

- Create a template similar to Figure 6.2 on page 73 with the main categories from the left side of your map in the first column of a spreadsheet.
- In the second column, insert the indicators from the left side and the right side of your map related to the categories.
- Put the heading, CEO, in the third column and people reporting to him or her in subsequent columns.
- Look at each indicator to determine who would own it as critical factors: CSF, CIF, CMF, or CIM. Repeat the process for the initiatives.

We refer to Figure 6.2 as the Accountability Template. It shows the indicators from the alignment map and the organizational structure. With this type of template, you are ready to ask questions

| Vision | Indicators or Initiatives | Brian Scott CEO | Business Unit CEOs | Shirin Chandra Planning | Pat Brown IT/R&D | Ted Finely CFO | Gail Locke HR | Lower levels |
|---|---|---|---|---|---|---|---|---|
| Xcorp Group Size | Indicator: $ Worldwide Sales | | | | | | | |
| | Initiative: Establish criteria for determining size, propose strategy for increasing size and coordinate with business units to implement | | | | | | | |
| | Initiative: Analyze existing potential for natural growth, propose growth segments, and coordinate with businesses to consult about implementation | | | | | | | |
| | Initiative: Execute existing planned acquisition in collaboration with finance and business leaders | | | | | | | |
| | Initiative: Develop & implement plan to maximize synergies to increase sales | | | | | | | |
| | Initiative: Establish acquisition criteria, develop plan and implement plan after approval by XCorp Group | | | | | | | |
| Image | Indicator: Top of mind | | | | | | | |
| | Initiative: Determine the desired Xcorp Group image, develop and implement a plan for promoting it after approval | | | | | | | |
| Coverage | Indicator: # of countries covered | | | | | | | |
| | Indicator: % of countries in #1 position | | | | | | | |
| | Initiative: Develop and implement a plan to maximize coverage | | | | | | | |

FIGURE 6.2 **Accountability Assignment for XCorp Group's Top Team**

to the participants in your meeting. Here are the questions you will need to put before them and facilitate conversation to arrive at consensus.

*Who has the greatest direct influence on this indicator, at the lowest level?*

For example, take the first entry in Figure 6.2 that is a process indicator, "$ worldwide sales." This question will cause people to think about who is actually selling. Someone will offer an answer, and others will either agree or offer different suggestions. Don't be surprised if it takes time to find the best answer. Some of the most valuable insights come from the consultation concerning who actually "owns" an indicator as a CSF. In the XCorp Group example, they decided that the indicator was the CSF of the salesperson within the business units (see Figure 6.3).

| Indicators or Initiatives | Brian Scott CEO | Business Unit CEOs | Shirin Chandra Planning | Pat Brown IT/R&D | Ted Finely CFO | Gail Locke HR | Lower Levels |
|---|---|---|---|---|---|---|---|
| Indicator: $ Worldwide sales | CMF | CMF | | | | | CSF |

FIGURE 6.3 **Accountability for Process Indicator**

*Who has the indispensable influence on this indicator?*

Once you have decided who owns this as CSF in the organization, you can answer this question. Actually, the CSF owner is the best person to identify who has indispensable influence on the factor. The answer would be that logistics, production, and the marketing manager would have indispensable influence on sales and therefore each will have a CIF within the business unit of the organization.

*Who has management influence?*

Your managers can answer this question. In the XCorp example they decided that "$ sales" was a CMF for Brian and the managers in between him and the owner of the CSF. Your managers might decide that the CMF assignment can be at the sales manager level within the business unit only and not any levels above.

*Who had dotted line influence?*

For dotted line influence, let's take another indicator "percent reduction in undesirable turnover within the group." If you have dotted line reporting in your company, you can answer this question. In the XCorp example, the HR area had dotted line influence on the HR functions of the four businesses. Therefore the assignment of roles looked like the following Figure 6.4 on page 75.

The same type of conversation will be necessary to determine accountability for initiative indicators. You ask similar questions as

| Indicators or Initiatives | Brian Scott CEO | Business Unit CEOs | Shirin Chandra Planning | Pat Brown IT/R&D | Ted Finely CFO | Gail Locke HR | Lower Levels |
|---|---|---|---|---|---|---|---|
| Indicator: % reduction in undesirable turnover within the Group | | | | | | CIM | CSF |

FIGURE 6.4 **Example of Dotted Line Influence**

listed above. For example for "establish criteria for determining size, propose strategy for increasing size, and coordinate with business units to implement," you ask, "who has the greatest direct influence on this initiative at the highest appropriate level?" The participants will think about this and consult to arrive at a consensus. In the XCorp Group example, they decided that it belonged as INX for Shirin Chandra, the director of planning with INIs to the business unit CEOs, Pat Brown, the IT director, and Ted Finley, the CFO as shown in Figure 6.5.

| Indicators or Initiatives | Brian Scott CEO | Business Unit CEOs | Shirin Chandra Planning | Pat Brown IT/R&D | Ted Finely CFO | Gail Locke HR | Lower Levels |
|---|---|---|---|---|---|---|---|
| Initiative: Establish criteria for determining size, propose strategy for increasing size, and coordinate with business units to implement. | | INI | INX | INI | INI | | |

FIGURE 6.5 **Example of Accountability for Initiatives**

Once you arrive at a consensus about the ownership of the CSFs, CIFs, and CMFs, you enter them in your template. By the time you have done this exercise with two or three indicators, everyone will be conversant with the methodology and the process will go faster. In Figure 6.6 on page 76, we used our fictional company, XCorp, as an example so you can see how this accountability structure might look.

As you see in this example, the XCorp Group was assigning accountability based on indicators and strategic initiatives from their alignment map. They decided that the CSFs for some of the indicators belonged to lower levels, within the business units. They

| Vision | Indicators or Initiatives | Brian Scott CEO | Business Unit CEOs | Shirin Chandra Planning | Pat Brown IT/R&D | Ted Finely CFO | Gail Locke HR | Lower levels |
|---|---|---|---|---|---|---|---|---|
| Xcorp Group Size | Indicator: $ Worldwide Sales | CMF | CMF | | | | | CSF |
| | Initiative: Establish criteria for determining size, propose strategy for increasing size and coordinate with business units to implement | | INI | INX | INI | INI | | |
| | Initiative:Analyze existing potential for natural growth, propose growth segments, and coordinate with businesses to consult about implementation | | INI | INX | INI | INI | | |
| | Initiative: Establish acquisition criteria, develop plan and implement plan after approval by XCorp Group | | INI | INX | | | | |
| | Initiative: Develop & implement plan to maximize synergies to increase sales | IMX | INX | | | | | |
| | Initiative: Execute existing planned acquisition in collaboration with finance and business leaders | | INX | | | INI | | |
| Image | Indicator: Top of mind | | | | | | | CSF |
| | Initiative: Determine the desired Xcorp Group image, develop and implement a plan for promoting it after approval | | | INX | | | | |
| Coverage | Indicator: # of countries covered | | CMF | | | | | CSF |
| | Indicator: % of countries in #1 position | | | | | | | CSF |
| | Initiative: Develop and implement a plan to maximize coverage | IMX | INX | INI | | | | |

FIGURE 6.6 **Accountability Assignment for XCorp Group's Top Team—Page 1**

assigned accountability to the individuals who were participating in the offsite, but left the assignment within the business units to occur at the business unit level.

If your company is small, then you have less complexity in terms of the number of vision indicators or initiatives. Nevertheless, the questions can help identify where accountability lies both for the indicators and the initiatives.

| Vision | Indicators or Initiatives | Brian Scott CEO | Business Unit CEOs | Shirin Chandra Planning | Pat Brown IT/R&D | Ted Finely CFO | Gail Locke HR | Lower levels |
|---|---|---|---|---|---|---|---|---|
| Excellent treatment of employees | Indicator: # of qualified applicants for vacant positions within Xcorp Group | | CIF | | | | CSF | |
| | Indicator: % reduction in undesirable turnover within the group | | | | | | CIM | CSF |
| | Indicator: Climate survey index average for the Group | | | | | | CIF | CSF |
| | Initiative: Develop and implement plan to transfer best human resource practices to all businesses to attract & retain talent | | | | | | INX | |
| | Initiative: Plan and implement processes to spread the Group values of excelence across businesses | | | | | | INX | |
| Outstanding value for shareholders | Indicator: Economic Value Added (EVA) | CSF | CSF | | | CIF | | |
| | Indicator: Market Value Added (MVA) | | CSF | | | CIF | | |
| | Indicator: Earnings Per Share (EPS) | CSF | CSF | | | CIF | | |
| Social Responsibility | Group Social Responsibility score | | CSF | | | | | |
| Innovations | Initiative: Establish and operate fund to provide financial support to businesses for developing new products or services for their markets | | INI | | | INX | | |

FIGURE 6.6  **Accountability Assignment for XCorp Group's Top Team—Page 2**

---

➤ **THE NEXT STEPS** ◄ ———————

You are now ready to take the accountability you have defined and learn how to apply it to individual scorecards. The scorecards you create will enable everyone to focus on their own contribution to the success of the company.

# CHAPTER 7

# The Scorecard

B rian's team is moving on to the next step of the total alignment process. Using the accountability that was defined for each indicator in the alignment map, the team members build individual scorecards for each job, clarifying individual responsibilities and considering cross-functional collaboration. You will learn this valuable process and how to apply it to your company.

## → THE CASE STUDY ←

The XCorp Group executives were now ready to see how all of the work they had done on defining accountability would translate into scorecards. Everyone was familiar with business scorecards that measure the performance of a business or department. But, the idea of a scorecard measuring individual performance was new to most of them. In fact, they were somewhat skeptical about how individual scorecards would be received by their organization. The Infoman explained that when the individual scorecards are well defined, they are welcomed. Why? Because individuals understand how they are contributing to the success of the organization. The individual scorecard provides clarity. It aligns the efforts of each person with the vision and strategy of the organization. It focuses the individual on those aspects of their job that will have the most direct impact.

| Vision Elements | Critical Factors or Initiative Indexes | Role | Weight |
|---|---|---|---|
| | | | |
| | | | |
| | | | |
| | | | |
| | | | |

FIGURE 7.1  **Scorecard Template**

The Infoman showed the group a template for the individual scorecard with four columns. He explained that the first column is for the vision elements from the vision tree. The second column lists the critical factors and initiative indexes assigned to the individual. The third column clarifies the person's role related to the factors and initiative indexes. The fourth column shows the weight of importance as shown in Figure 7.1.

Based on the accountability conversations from the previous day, the group was able to fill this template out for each participant. Later, the business heads would engage their teams to apply the methodology and define individual scorecards for all the jobs in their pyramids of responsibility.

## ⟶ ALIGN IT: CONSTRUCTING INDIVIDUAL ⟵ SCORECARDS

Let's briefly review what you have learned in the last few chapters. In Chapter 2, you defined a mission and vision for your company. In Chapter 3, you measured the vision in terms of indicators and created a vision tree. In Chapter 4, you developed strategy and strategic initiatives and constructed a strategy tree. You linked your vision tree and strategy trees in Chapter 5 to construct an alignment map. In Chapter 6, you learned how to use the Alignment Map to assign accountability for the indicators and initiatives to the right person

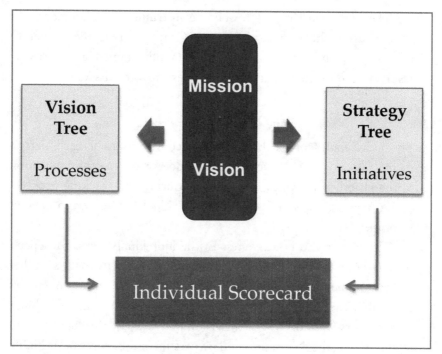

FIGURE 7.2  **Alignment of the Scorecard**

at the right level of your organization. And, you learned how each factor is influenced by the actions of several people.

Figure 7.2 illustrates this brief summary in a graphical form. It shows that the scorecard receives two types of metrics, from the left side and the right side of the Alignment Map. Having assigned accountability and the roles for the indicators explained in the last chapter, the scorecard is then created for each individual.

Now, let's learn how to put it all together to produce an individual scorecard for each person in your organization. *The purpose of all the previous chapters was to help you define the individual scorecard.* Why is the scorecard so important? Because the scorecard connects the person to vision and strategy, and when all the jobholders in a company have a scorecard, the entire company is aligned. With a scorecard defined clearly in measurable terms, and with specific roles identified, people will be focused on the most important activities. Accountability is clear.

The scorecard can be an ongoing instrument of alignment. We will be using the scorecard later in Chapter 11 as the trigger to initiate problem solving and action planning aimed at improving results that push the organization forward towards its vision.

### The Individual Scorecard

The individual scorecard defines the contribution of each person to the organization. It measures the added value to the realization of the vision. It provides a way of measuring and tracking progress on an ongoing basis and keeps the individual focused on important priorities.

The power and effectiveness of the individual scorecard depend to a large extent on each person taking ownership for his or her factors. Remember that the scorecard has a few important factors that are either critical success factors or influence factors. Since these factors were derived from vision and strategy through a sound methodology, the acceptance and ownership of the scorecard is highly probable. Nevertheless, to further increase the sense of personal ownership, it is recommended that you involve an individual from each job in constructing their scorecard from the alignment map. With involvement comes understanding, and understanding leads to positive action.

When you define individual scorecards in your organization, the first attempt could produce a large number of indicators, particularly for top managers. This is because many top managers feel the more indicators they have, the more important their job is. Many are reluctant to delegate to lower levels either because they are hesitant that the job won't get done, or they are reluctant to let go of control. There might be factors listed as CSFs that should really be CMFs and need to be delegated to lower levels, or just too many indicators that are not significant enough to be on their scorecards. In our experience, we have found that more than five factors is too many. This is because it is better to focus on three to five main factors and assure outstanding performance of these factors, than diffuse your focus on a large number of factors.

The way to reduce the factors on your scorecard is to delegate. Yet, it might be difficult for managers at first to delegate and let go. It might be difficult for them to rely on lower levels to take responsibility. However, as they begin delegating to competent lower levels they will realize that they will not need all the factors.

There is a story in Stephen Covey's book on *The 7 Habits of Highly Effective People* that is relevant to our discussion of individual scorecards. He gives an example of filling a jar with a few large stones, pebbles, sand, and water. He says that if you don't put the five big stones in the jar first, you would not be able to fit them in later. If you do put the five big stones first, then the pebbles, then the sand and then the water, all will fit. In our example, the five big stones are the five indicators and initiatives. They are on the scorecard because they need priority attention, because they are the main drivers of your vision. The pebbles, the sand, and the water are the many other priorities that fill your agendas. You can address these other priorities as well after focusing on the five.

While the individual scorecards have a few factors that define the accountability of the individual, business scorecards have as many factors as necessary to capture the performance of the business. Let's look more closely at the differences.

### *Business Scorecard/Individual Scorecard*

Look at the way you measure the success of your business. What do you look at? Probably the key numbers you would consider are financial such as the company's bank account, cash flow, receivables, payables, and profit. Additionally, you would look at how you are growing your customer base, how happy your customers are, and what value you are providing for them. You would look at the effectiveness of the processes you have in place to deliver your value proposition, and how you are managing your human capital. The indicators related to these would constitute your business scorecard. They will show the success of your business in these areas. Every business must carefully watch its business scorecard.

How does this type of business scorecard, developed by many companies, compare to the individual scorecards we are describing here? There are several important differences. Let's take a look.

- ➤ *Alignment with vision*. The alignment to the mission or vision is usually not clear in business scorecards. They are very clear in the individual scorecard as shown in Figure 7.1 on page 80.
- ➤ *Progress of strategic initiatives*. Strategic initiatives are tracked outside of business scorecards. They are tracked within the individual scorecard because the five indicators in the individual scorecard are usually a mix of vision indicators and strategy indicators.
- ➤ *Concept of roles for indicators*. The concept of roles for the indicators does not exist in business scorecards. It does in the individual scorecard and is there to encourage cross-functional collaboration.
- ➤ *Information in the scorecard*. Business scorecards include aggregate consolidated numbers; the individual scorecards show numbers from the source, where performance takes place.
- ➤ *Number of factors*. Business scorecards can have a large number of indicators; the individual scorecard focuses on a few.

We are not stating which is better, the business scorecard or the individual scorecard. We are simply stating their differences. Both are necessary, useful, and complementary. You should also track the performance of the business as a whole through a business scorecard. Following the methodology in this book, your business scorecard would include a list of all the indicators on the left side of your alignment map. Watching the status of those indicators on a monthly or quarterly basis will be necessary to help you to see how your company is moving towards its vision.

### *A Shift in Paradigm*

Let's examine the two triangles in Figure 7.3 on page 85. Suppose the triangles represent your pyramid of human resources engaged in the present operations of your company and building its future.

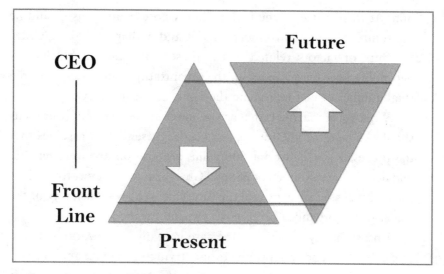

FIGURE 7.3 **Attention to the Present vs. the Future**

The triangles correspond to the left and right side of your alignment map.

The triangle on the left shows a focus on the present; the triangle on the right shows a focus on the future. The height of each triangle represents the levels of management you have in your company. The distance from the CEO to the front line could be far in some companies and flat in others. If you are a small company, you could have two to three levels at most. In larger companies, there could be five or more levels. The more levels you have the more meaningful this shift in paradigm will be.

Naturally, more people are working close to the front-line than at the upper levels of the organization. When you assign accountability for indicators from the left and right side of your alignment map to people in your pyramid, each individual will have a mix of accountability for the present and the future on their scorecard.

Let us draw a horizontal line through the two triangles close to the front line, as shown in Figure 7.3. The main accountability for this individual will be the indicators of the present processes. He will have several CSFs and perhaps no INXs. This person should be mainly focused on his contribution to existing processes delegated to him. At the other extreme is the CEO, whose main focus should be the future. She will have mostly INXs and perhaps a CSF or CMF. The mix of factors related to the present and the future changes depending on where you are in the organizational hierarchy, but the total number of factors remain the same, about five factors.

What we are saying is that as you move up the pyramid your focus should be more on the future, less on the present. This assumes that the processes for delivering the value proposition are well defined, and delegated to competent people. Give them the support to do their job and focus on strategy and the future. It is the responsibility of the leader of the organization to have a vision for the future.

Unfortunately, this is not the case in many organizations. Often upper levels spend far too much time trying to manage the present. By doing so, they could interfere with the right people doing their job. When the top levels spend their energy focusing on the future, they will advance the company faster towards the vision, will be more aware of the changing environment in their markets, and will be able ensure better execution of their strategies. The application of this one principle could have a great positive impact on your company.

## ⟶ APPLY IT: BUILD YOUR TEAM AND ⟵ COMPANY SCORECARDS

Assuming that you have defined accountability for your job holders as explained in the last chapter, you will have produced a spreadsheet similar to Figure 6.6 on page 76. To summarize, this spreadsheet lists the main branches of your vision tree in the first column and the indicators of process and initiatives in the second column. The third column heading has your name if you are the CEO. The column headings in the fourth column onwards are the names of people reporting to you directly. The last column heading is, "lower levels."

As discussed in the last chapter, the roles of people related to each indicator in this spreadsheet are clearly identified as CSF, CMF, etc. The entries in any of the columns of this spreadsheet (Figure 6.6) from Column 3 onwards, will make up the individual scorecard for the person.

Let's see how the process was applied at the XCorp Group, and examine how Brian Scott's scorecard emerges from Figure 6.6 Brian and his team reviewed the accountability template. There were five factors and initiative indexes for Brian in the third column. They copied them onto the scorecard template shown in Figure 7.1 on page 80. Then there was conversation about the CEO position and the most important aspects of the job in order to determine the weighting of the factors. When they finished, Brian's scorecard looked like that in Figure 7.4.

## The Weighting Concept

The relative emphasis Brian puts on his five factors is defined by the weights in the last column. At any level, the assignment of weights will enable the individual to focus even more on where he should spend his time. How is the weighting done? A conversation takes place between each person and his boss. Together they agree on the weights. If you are the top person, your team can help you or you might need input from your board. The following criteria should be used to determine the weighting.

| Vision Elements | Critical Factors or Initiative Indexes | Role | Weight |
|---|---|---|---|
| XCorp Group Size | Worldwide Sales in Billions USD | CMF | 20 |
| | Develop and implement plan to maximize synergies to increase sales | IMX | 20 |
| Coverage | Develop and implement a plan to maximize coverage worldwide | IMX | 10 |
| Outstanding Value for Shareholders | EVA in Billions USD | CSF | 30 |
| | EPS | CSF | 20 |

FIGURE 7.4 **Scorecard for Brian Scott**

➤ The importance of the indicator of vision that has translated to a factor in the scorecard.

➤ The type of role the individual has related to the factor. If it is a CSF, it means that the factor is capturing the unique added value of the job. Therefore, more weight could be given to this indicator.

➤ The degree of impact the individual has on the factor in his role. For example, a CSF owner might have a lion share of influence among the team of his CIF owners, or slightly more impact than the others, which would be reflected in the weight.

These three criteria will enable the individual and the boss to discuss and arrive at a consensus on distributing 100 points among the factors in the scorecard.

If you are an entrepreneurial firm scaling up or a large firm growing your business rapidly, you will have to pay systematic attention to the processes that deliver your value proposition. The scorecards described in this chapter will be your ticket to success. They will guarantee that the right people are taking care of all that is important for your customers and for your company profitability. With this peace of mind you will have time to focus on the future of your company, which includes reading the market, staying in touch with the evolving needs of your customers, and the intentions of your competitors and their initiatives. You will be able to assure a healthy future for your company.

───────────────── ➤ **THE NEXT STEPS** ◄ ─────────────────

What happens when every job in your company has a well-defined scorecard? Your people will have clarity and will focus on delivering results. To benefit from the power of alignment you have already established, you will need a good follow up mechanism to assure continuing attention to the scorecards and sustaining the alignment already established. You will need a system. In the next chapter you will learn what that system looks like.

# CHAPTER 8

# Three One-Page Reports

Paying attention to the scorecard performance assumes high priority, and prompts the team to adopt a reporting system that provides accurate up-to-date data and performance transparency at all levels of the organization. You will learn how to create three one-page reports that will allow you to track your progress towards your vision.

## THE CASE STUDY

PAUL HARRIS was assigned to be the project manager of Total Alignment at XCorp Group. He was enthusiastic about his assignment and happy to be reporting directly to Brian. Paul had been motivated by his experience in the offsite sessions and was committed to the process.

Paul learned that the key to making alignment a reality was to populate the scorecards with accurate information updated on a regular basis: quarterly, monthly, weekly, or daily. Paul knew that the report would have to be backed up with accurate and reliable data drawn from existing data sources.

He worked with the company's information technology (IT) department to set up a system to produce the regular reports for managers. They called the scorecard report the Focus Report. The IT department arranged for the Focus Reports to be populated with information from the company data warehouse. The report would also provide the actual status of performance of all the indicators in the individual scorecard for the reporting period. Two further reports were developed: the Feedback Report, which gives each person the positive and negative exceptions from their Focus Report, and the Management Report, which highlights the positive and negative exceptions from within each manager's pyramid of responsibility.

# ➤ ALIGN IT: USING ACCURATE REPORTING TO ◄ TRACK ALIGNMENT

The reporting system described in the story is based on our book, *One Page Management* (www.totalalignment.com/opm). This system describes the structure of three reports for each individual: Focus, Feedback, and Management. The set of three reports is ideal for tracking alignment in the organization. Let's take a closer look at what those three reports can do for you and your teams.

## *The Focus Report*

The Focus Report shows the performance of the scorecard you developed in the last chapter. A sample of the Focus Report is shown in Figure 8.1 on page 91. This performance relates to the actual status of each of your indicators. The "status" of your indicator is the number that shows the result of the indicator in the previous period. For example, suppose the indicator in your scorecard is "percent customer returns" and the percentage of returns in the month of April was 3 percent. Then, the status for this indicator in your May Focus Report would show your performance to be 3 percent in the status column. Your status lets you know how you are performing so that you can align your efforts to improve the indicator.

When your status is evaluated against some agreed-upon criteria, then you will be able to determine if it was "good" or "bad." We like to use goals to establish those criteria. So, for each critical factor in your scorecard, you will establish three goal levels: minimum, satisfactory, and outstanding as shown in the template Figure 8.1.

| Vision Elements | Critical Success Factors or Initiatives | Type | Weight | Status | Min/ Max Goal | Satisfactory Goal | Outstanding Goal | Trend |
|---|---|---|---|---|---|---|---|---|
| | | | | | | | | |
| | | | | | | | | |
| | | | | | | | | |
| | | | | | | | | |
| | | | | | | | | |

FIGURE 8.1 Focus Report Template

The minimum goal is the level below whichever performance is not acceptable. Satisfactory is the level that would cause you to feel good about your performance and outstanding is the level of excellence.

Notice that for some factors, such as "number of units produced," more is better. For some other factors, such as "percent of scrap," less is better. This is the reason the heading in the sixth column says, "Min or Max goal." This way, you can identify acceptable performance as being higher than the minimum level or lower than the maximum level depending on the factor type. With these criteria you can determine three scenarios:

1. Excellent performance when the status is better than the outstanding goal.
2. Good performance or positive exception when your status is better than the satisfactory goal.
3. Bad performance or negative exception when your status is worse than the minimum goal.

In addition to the "status" and "goals," another important information is the "trend." The trend shows whether your status is getting better or worse. For example, your performance last month could be worse than the minimum, but the trend over the last five periods could be good. Conversely, your performance last month could be better than satisfactory, but the trend could be bad. This is useful information. You can determine the trend for each indicator by plotting the status of the indicator each month on a graph similar to the one we provide in Figure 8.2.

You can construct your own Focus Report by using the template in Figure 8.1, listing the indicators from your scorecard in the second column and the vision element they support in the first column. In the third column, insert the type of role you have with respect to the factor, CSF, CIF, etc. Then, in the fourth column, you can insert the weights for the factors you agreed on with your boss. Put your status for the last period in the fifth column, followed by the three goal levels in columns six through eight. Column nine is for trend information. Here, insert "G" for a good/positive trend, "B" for a

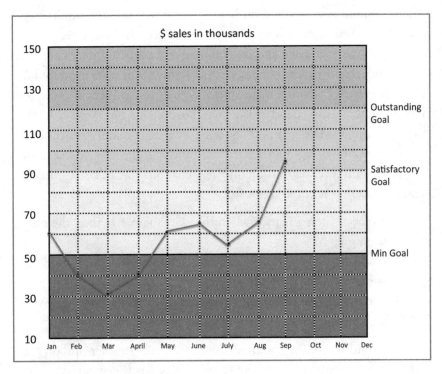

FIGURE 8.2 **Performance Graph**

bad or negative trend and "-" for no trend that comes from your analysis of the plot on the graph as we explained above. For example, you would put "G" for good trend in the September Focus Report for the indicator "$ sales in thousands" corresponding to the graph in Figure 8.2. We think you'll find that constructing your own Focus Report is a rewarding exercise. It allows you to reflect more deeply on your factors, the formula that defines them, the data that goes into their calculation, and the positive action they will require. You might be surprised at how useful the exercise is.

### The Feedback Report

The second one-page report is called the Feedback Report. This report is a summary of the "good news" and the "bad news" based on the status of your indicators. It illustrates the factors that have fallen below the unacceptable range in status and those that are above the satisfactory level. Those that fall in between the two are considered in the acceptable range. A template for the Feedback Report is shown in Figure 8.3.

| Good News—You've Made Your Goals | | | | | | |
|---|---|---|---|---|---|---|
| Critical Factors | Type | Status | Satisfactory Goal | Number of Periods in a Row | Exception Reported to | Trend |
|  |  |  |  |  |  |  |
|  |  |  |  |  |  |  |
|  |  |  |  |  |  |  |
| You Have Problems—Think of a Creative Solution | | | | | | |
| Critical Factors | Type | Status | Min/Max Goal | Number of Periods in a Row | Exception Reported to | Trend |
|  |  |  |  |  |  |  |
|  |  |  |  |  |  |  |
|  |  |  |  |  |  |  |

FIGURE 8.3  **Feedback Report Template**

This report also illustrates the number of time periods in a row that the factor has been better than the satisfactory goal or worse than the Min/Max goal. At a glance, you can see the feedback on your performance. Now, try constructing your own Feedback Report. Look at each factor in your Focus Report and compare your status with the goals. If it is better than the satisfactory goal, then put the factor along with its type, status, and the satisfactory goal, in the upper portion of the chart illustrated in Figure 8.3. If it is worse than the Min/Max goal, you can put the factor, type, status, and the Min/Max goal in the bottom half of the report in Figure 8.3. In the fifth column, enter how many times in a row this factor has performed better than the satisfactory goal or worse than the Min/Max goal.

## The Management Report

If you are a manager, you will need to know the reality of what is happening in your pyramid of responsibility, from the bottom up and the top down. To do this, one option would be to study the individual Focus Reports of those who report to you directly and indirectly. This could be time consuming and inefficient. To give you performance info in a more useful way, we have created a third report, the Management Report, that gives you a quick overview of the highlights of the Feedback Reports of everyone in your pyramid of responsibility, people reporting to you directly as well as indirectly.

This approach is management by exception. What does that mean? People who are performing within the acceptable range won't show up on this report—they are doing satisfactory work and, at this time, you have little need to address their individual performance. But the star performers as well as those who are having challenges will show up. You are looking for the exceptions on either end of the performance spectrum in this report. Obviously, reporting all the exceptions in the Management Report would crowd this report and diminish its effectiveness. Therefore, an escalation scheme is embedded in the reporting system to determine what exceptions get reported upwards.

Based on an escalation rule that is customizable, positive and negative exceptions rise when they are recurring. The rule we recommend is two or more consecutive exceptions worse than the Min/Max level or above the satisfactory level to start climbing to the next level. Beyond that, the speed of escalation upwards depends on the importance of the factor. Some can go up quickly to the next level after three consecutive exceptions and some more slowly.

The rationale for the escalation rule is that, for example, a supervisor who has a problem with returns might have a short time to resolve it. If he doesn't, then notice of the problem is escalated. The boss has a predetermined length of time to help him fix it. If the problem continues, then the next level up is alerted and so on up the line. If this is a severe problem, and no one seems to have the answer, then the top person in the organization finds out about it. It is most likely a systemic issue that is outside the control of the supervisor who is receiving the blame. When the problem shows up on your Management Report, you know that everyone has attempted to solve it. Now you have the opportunity to intervene and get the issue resolved.

You will also get the good news. Often in organizations the boss takes credit for the outstanding performance of a person reporting to him. With the Management Report, performance is transparent. Outstanding performance is reported upwards and the right person is recognized.

## Data for the Scorecards

Your scorecard has either critical factors or initiative indexes or both. Each factor will have a formula with one or more variables. The data for each variable will come from your current data systems. Some will be automated and some might be manual. When the source of data for each variable is identified, then the computer accesses that source, calculates the status using the formula, and displays it as the status of the critical factor on the Focus Report. If you are a small company, it is possible to create these reports manually. You identify the sources of data for each variable, access the source on a regular basis, obtain the data related to the variables, and calculate the status of your critical factors.

As we discussed in Chapter 5, the Initiative Index or INX is a number based on the evaluation of the customers of the initiative. The evaluation is converted to a number and is displayed as the status of the INX in the Focus Report. Refer to Figure 5.3 on page 63 in Chapter 5 for the illustration of how the initiative is evaluated and the data produced.

## Producing the Scorecards

You can construct any of these three reports manually using spreadsheets. However, if your organization is large, then you would prefer to have the reports produced by a software linked to your data systems. There is a specific software tool designed for Total Alignment, which is available from our website at www.totalalignment.com/tops.

## ➤ APPLY IT: CUSTOMIZE YOUR FOCUS, FEEDBACK, ◄ AND MANAGEMENT REPORTS

Let's look at examples of each of the templates for the reports with information in them using the XCorp case study. The vision elements and critical factors come from the scorecards of XCorp. The data is not from a real company. It is used here to illustrate how the Feedback Report is derived from the Focus Report. The reports shown below belong to two people from opposite ends of the XCorp organization, Brian Scott and Arnold Turner.

### *The Focus Report*

Each person who has a scorecard will have a Focus Report. In Chapter 7, we used Brian Scott's scorecard as an example. It had only the name of the factor or initiative, the type, and the weight. Now as it is becoming his Focus Report, the status, the goals, and the trend

| Vision Elements | Critical Factors or Initiatives | Type | Weight | Status | Min/Max Goal | Satisfactory Goal | Outstanding Goal | Trend |
|---|---|---|---|---|---|---|---|---|
| XCorp Group size | Woldwide sales in billions USD | CMF | 20 | 0.85 | 0.9 | 1.2 | 1.4 | None |
| XCorp Group size | Develop plan to maximize synergies to increase sales | IMX | 20 | 87 | 85 | 90 | 95 | None |
| Coverage | Develop plan to maximize coverage worldwide | IMX | 10 | 80 | 85 | 90 | 95 | None |
| Out-standing value for share-holders | EVA in billions USD | CSF | 30 | 0.04 | 0.02 | 0.03 | 0.10 | Good |
| Out-standing value for share-holders | EPS | CSF | 20 | 30 | 35 | 40 | 50 | None |

FIGURE 8.4 **Focus Report for Brian Scott—Period Ending June 30th**

are added to the picture. This is how his report looks now (see Figure 8.4). This is a sample that you can use as an example for your own Focus Report.

Let's look at a Focus Report for another person at XCorp, someone far removed from Brian Scott, the CEO. His name is Arnold Turner, a foreman in one of XCorp's manufacturing plants. Figure 8.5 on page 98 shows Turner's Focus Report.

| Vision Components | Critical Factors or Initiatives | Type | Weight | Status | Min or Max Goal | Satisfactory Goal | Outstanding Goal | Trend |
|---|---|---|---|---|---|---|---|---|
| XCorp Group Size | Number of units produced (000) | CSF | 35 | 660 | 450 | 600 | 750 | None |
| Operational Effectiveness | Percent of scrap | CSF | 20 | 0.1 | 1.0 | 0.5 | 0 | Good |
| Operational Effectiveness | Percent of machine downtime | CSF | 15 | 2.0 | 4.0 | 1.5 | 1.0 | None |
| Satisfactory Value of shareholders | Percent of overtime | CSF | 15 | 3.2 | 3.0 | 2.0 | 0.0 | None |
| Outstanding value for Customers | Percent of products returned | CSF | 15 | 0.1 | 1.5 | 0.3 | 0 | None |

FIGURE 8.5  Focus Report for Arnold Turner—Period Ending June 30th

Arnold has a mix of factors. For some factors, such as "number of units produced," more is better. For some other factors, such as "percent of scrap," less is better.

### The Feedback Report

You will also need a Feedback Report for each person who has a Focus Report. Figure 8.6 is an example of Brian's Feedback Report with the positive and negative exceptions separated into two sections. The actual status of each row of the Focus Report has been analyzed against the goals by the software. If the status was better than the satisfactory goal, it appeared on the top of the Feedback Report and if it was worse than the minimum level, it appeared on the bottom.

Notice that the report includes the number of consecutive periods of exception and whether the exception had been reported to upper

| Good News—You've Made Your Goals | | | | | | |
|---|---|---|---|---|---|---|
| Critical Success Factor | Type | Status | Satisfactory Goal | Number of Periods in a Row | Exception Reported to | Trend |
| EVA in billions of USD | CSF | 0.04 | 0.03 | 2 | The Board | Good |
| | | | | | | |
| | | | | | | |

| You Have Problems—Think of a Creative Solution | | | | | | |
|---|---|---|---|---|---|---|
| Critical Success Factor | Type | Status | Min/Max Goal | Number of Periods in a Row | Exception Reported to | Trend |
| Sales total in billion of USD | CMF | 0.85 | 0.9 | 1 | No one | No |
| EPS | CSF | 30 | 35 | 1 | No one | No |
| Identify and implement a plan to maximize coverage worldwide | IMX | 80 | 85 | 1 | No one | No |

FIGURE 8.6 Feedback Report for Brian Scott—Period ending June 30th

levels in the organization. In the case of Brian, one factor with two consecutive exceptions was reported up to the Board.

The Feedback Report of Arnold Turner is constructed in the same way as shown in Figure 8.7 on page 100. In the sixth column you see the names of Arnold's upper managers listed. Joe Bosco is Arnold's immediate boss. Joe reports to John Erdman, who reports to Tom Brown. Arnold has one negative exception listed in the lower half of his Feedback Report "percent of overtime." It has been worse than the minimum for two consecutive periods, and therefore is reported to his boss.

As you see, the same rule applies to his positive "percent products returned," which has been better than his satisfactory goal for twice

| Good News—You've Made Your Goals | | | | | | |
|---|---|---|---|---|---|---|
| Critical Factors or Initiatives | Type | Status | Satisfactory Goal | Number of Periods in a Row | Exception Reported to | Trend |
| Number of units produced (000) | CSF | 660.00 | 600.00 | 6 | Tom Brown | None |
| Percent of scrap | CSF | 0.10 | 0.50 | 10 | Brian Scott | Good |
| Percent of products returned | CSF | 0.10 | 0.30 | 2 | Joe Bosco | None |
| You Have Problems—Think of a Creative Solution | | | | | | |
| Critical Factors or Initiatives | Type | Status | Minimum or Maximum Goal | Number of Periods in a Row | Exception Reported to | Trend |
| Percent of overtime | CSF | 3.2 | 3.0 | 2 | Joe Bosco | No |

FIGURE 8.7 **Feedback Report for Arnold Turner—Period Ending June 30th**

in a row and is also reported to his boss. His indicator, "number of units produced," has been in the positive exception six times in a row and is reported up to Tom Brown, the vice president of manufacturing. And finally, his "percent of scrap" has been better than his satisfactory goal for ten periods and is reported up to Brian Scott, the CEO.

## The Management Report

The Management Report receives the positive and negative exceptions coming from the lower levels in the manager's pyramid of

| People Indirectly Reporting to You<br>Several Levels Below | People Directly Reporting to You<br>One Level Below |
|---|---|
| Zone 1: Positive<br>Highlights of Excellent Performance of People<br>Several Levels Below | Zone 2: Positive<br>Highlights and Details of Good Performance<br>of Direct Reports |
| Zone 3: Negative<br>Highlights of Chronic Performance Problems<br>Several Levels Below | Zone 4: Negative<br>Highlights and Details of Problem Performance<br>of Direct Reports |

FIGURE 8.8  **Management Report Structure**

responsibility. Not all exceptions are reported upwards, only those according to the escalation criteria.

Take a look at Figure 8.8, which is the structure of the Management Report. It has four zones that are grouped into two sections. Zones 1 and 2 are positive exceptions. Zones 3 and 4 are negative exceptions. The right side of the report is exceptions from direct reports. The left side is exceptions from indirect reports.

To understand the example of Brian Scott's Management Report, take a look at Figure 8.9, the organizational chart for XCorp Group. Brian has eight people reporting to him, four business CEOs and four staff directors.

Figure 8.10, on page 102, is Brian's Management Report showing the four zones. The exceptions from his direct collaborators are listed on the right side of this report. The left side shows the star performers and problem areas from people reporting to any

FIGURE 8.9  **Organizational Chart for XCorp Group**

| Good News from Several Levels Below | | | Good News from One Level Below | | | | | | |
|---|---|---|---|---|---|---|---|---|---|
| Name | Critical Factors or Initiatives | Number of Periods in a Row | Name | Critical Factors or Initiatives | Type | Status | Satisfactory Goal | Number of Periods in a Row | Trend |
| John Daley | Customer Satisfaction Index— XCorp US | 8 | Don Turner, TechCorp | EVA TechCorp | CSF | 0.026 | 0.025 | 3 | Good |
| Arnold Turner | $ Scrap XCorp US | 10 | Christine Adams, IES | Percent of growth in repeat sales | CMF | 25 | 20 | 5 | Good |
| Challenges in Several Levels Below | | | Challenges in One Level Below | | | | | | |
| Name | Critical Factors or Initiatives | Number of Periods in a Row | Name | Critical Factors or Initiatives | Type | Status | Min/Max Goal | Number of Periods in a Row | Trend |
| Kit Bowers | Sales NE Region— XCorp US | 7 | Shirin Chandra | Analyze existing natural growth potential | INX | 75 | 85 | 3 | No |
| Tony Rowe | Customer Satisfaction Index, IES | 10 | Ted Finley | Establish and operate a fund to provide financial support to businesses for developing new products or services for their markets | INX | 78 | 85 | 4 | Bad |

FIGURE 8.10  **Management Report for Brian Scott—Period Ending June 30th**

one of his direct reports. These exceptions have been recurring with sufficient frequency to satisfy the escalation rule and show up on the report of the CEO.

While the organizational chart shows eight people reporting to Brian, only four names appear on the right side of this report. This is because the factors on the Focus Reports of the other four people are performing in the expected zone, that is, between Min/Max and satisfactory levels. Also, if there were positive or negative exceptions in their Feedback Reports, the exceptions could have been first-time exceptions, and therefore would not climb to his level.

Note that John Daley and Arnold Turner are clearly outstanding performers and are people who should be recognized by the CEO. Arnold Turner had seen Brian's name on his Feedback Report, indicating that his good performance was being reported to Brian. The Management Report for Brian shows that excellent performance on the upper left zone. Brian should investigate their situation and reward Arnold and John accordingly. Tony Rowe and Kit Bowers clearly have some chronic issues, which warrant further investigation and attention.

There is a tremendous power in this Management Report for strengthening the organization. When a manager pays attention and takes appropriate action on each of the exceptions in the four zones, that action influences the behavior of individuals. For example, when a manager sees a positive exception on his Management Report and picks up the phone to express his satisfaction to the person responsible, that reinforcement will release a positive energy that sustains that good performance. It can carry over to other people who were also responsible for that good performance and could even carry over to improve other indicators. When a manager sees a negative exception on his Management Report and investigates why it is recurring, this enables the right people to be able to focus on and solve the problem.

The series of three reports described in this chapter provides a complete overview that focuses every person on his or her accountability, encourages cross-functional problem solving at every level, and provides transparency of performance giving credit to those star performers in the organization.

## THE NEXT STEPS

The next few chapters will show you how each individual can use these three reports to improve their own results. The next chapter is about improving individual skills that are the foundation for delegation and empowerment.

# CHAPTER 9

# Aligning Competency

I n the story, the XCorp Human Resource managers become aware
that just as the scorecards focus individuals on specific indicators,
competency must focus individuals on specific core skills aligned
with their indicators. You will learn how a systematic process for
aligning competency with the scorecards is the key to moving the
organization forward towards its vision.

## ➤ THE CASE STUDY ◄

GAIL LOCKE, XCorp Group's Human Resources director, arrived in Chicago to chair a conference of HR
managers from the four businesses of the Group. The purpose was to discuss competency. She was
accompanied by Jane Baker, a colleague of the Infoman.

The participants were aware of the progress achieved so far in the alignment process. The mission and
vision of the XCorp Group were clear and inspiring. The map of alignment was available for everyone to
view and to see how they were contributing to the forward progress of the company. Individual scorecards
had been defined to establish clear accountability, and a reporting system was being put in place to give

each person feedback information on his or her performance as well as the performance of those they managed. They were well positioned to begin using these advances to impact results, which is the main purpose of alignment.

Jane explained that a big factor for impacting results was competency. Improving results means improving the factors in Focus Reports and to do that each person needs to improve competency in the skills aligned with their scorecards. She reminded them that when competency improves, performance improves. The reverse might not be true. If performance improves, it doesn't necessarily mean that competency has improved. Many other factors could be involved such as a change in environment, someone else's actions, or an outside factor like fluctuation in currency values.

Improving competency requires identifying the skills needed, evaluating the level of competency in each, and then pursuing a plan to improve competency in those skills. Each individual needs to do this, and the HR managers need to support them in the process. Jane described to the group how the competency improvement process can begin and cascade through the organization.

## ⟶ ALIGN IT: ESTABLISHING AND MEASURING ◄⟶ CRITERIA FOR COMPETENCY

You know that the competency of your people is a huge factor in your success as a company. When you hired the managers and other employees, you no doubt picked the best talent. What criteria did you use? Probably education, experience, and attitude were among your top criteria. But after hiring, would you say that your people are highly competent? Actually, we should rephrase this commonly used statement because asking if a person is highly competent is, in fact, confusing. The question is, "In what areas are they highly competent?" For example, a person could be highly competent in using Excel spreadsheets but poor in conducting a marketing campaign. So, what criteria do you use to determine if a person is highly competent in the skills required for their job? Here are some ideas to consider:

➤ How well and how fast is the person able to apply the skill needed for the job?

➤ Can the person maintain the quality and speed consistently and under adverse conditions?

➤ Can the person produce results by using this skill with minimum effort?

➤ Can the person apply the skills effectively alone, without supervision?

People often look great on their bios and could have been a good performer in their former position but perform poorly in your company. If you have such employees, how do you improve their performance? Sending them to courses on various important general topics is often not sufficient. *To improve performance, competencies must be aligned with scorecards.* To accomplish this, help your employees define the skills required for their job, assist them in evaluating their level of competency in these skills and support them in their plans for improving them. In this book, this is what competency is all about.

## *Identification of the Required Skills*

When you study your scorecard, think about what repeated actions are needed to enable you to drive your factors to the outstanding level. Then, organize those actions into logical groups and assign a title to each group. The title identifies the skill, and the repeated actions are the descriptors of the skill. Let's take an example. If you are in the human resources department and your job is to interview job applicants, one of the factors in your scorecard is "percent of successful interviews." The repeated actions related to this factor are:

➤ Analyzing the candidate's bio
➤ Formulating relevant questions
➤ Creating a relaxed environment
➤ Recognizing talent
➤ Determining the candidate's fit into the culture of the job
➤ Explaining the requirements of the job clearly

These would be the descriptors of a skill set you could call "interviewing skills." When you apply these actions as an interviewer, you will increase the probability of finding the right talent to recommend. Some results from applying those descriptors might look like this:

➤ You have analyzed the candidate's bio and determined whether the candidate's background and experience should fit the needs of the job.

➤ You have asked relevant questions to better understand the bio.

➤ You have created an environment that encourages the candidate to be authentic.

➤ You have recognized the talent and determined that the candidate would also embrace the culture of the organization.

➤ You have explained clearly what the job entails.

➤ Using skillset descriptors to yield these results will give the candidate accurate information on which he or she can base their decision to accept or reject the job offer. Improving competency in "interviewing skills," will enable you to improve the indicator in your Focus Report, "percent of successful interviews."

### *Evaluating Competency*

There are many techniques for skill evaluation, and many of them could work. Here is a simple and effective approach that we recommend. It is based on two variables: effort and supervision. A person is fully competent in a skill when he or she can perform a task with quality, with less effort than is required by a standard performer in the industry, and with minimal supervision. On the flip side, when a great deal of effort is needed to perform a task with quality, and a high degree of supervision is required, the person has a low degree of competency.

The evaluation of the "extent of effort" and "degree of supervision" can be done using the form in Figure 9.1 on page 109. The level of effort expended by the person is evaluated on a scale of very high, high, medium, or low, and the level of supervision required is evaluated on a scale of continuous, frequent, occasional, or never.

| | | Critical Skill |
|---|---|---|
| YOUR NAME: _____ | | |
| YOUR BOSS'S NAME: _____ | | |
| DATE OF EVALUATION: _____ | | |

| **A:** | **EXTENT OF EFFORT** | Check One |
|---|---|---|
| 1) | My direct report has to work twice as hard on this skill to achieve the same satisfactory results compared to the standard performer in the industry. | ☐ Very High |
| 2) | My direct report has to work harder than the standard performer to get the same satisfactory results. | ☐ High |
| 3) | My direct report has to work just as hard as the standard performer to achieve the same satisfactory results. | ☐ Medium |
| 4) | My direct report can achieve the same satisfactory results with less effort than the standard performer. | ☐ Low |

| **B:** | **EXTENT OF SUPERVISION** | Check One |
|---|---|---|
| 1) | My direct report must check with me or an expert to be sure each step of the way is performed with quality. | ☐ Continuous |
| 2) | My direct report needs me or an expert to be available to review major steps. | ☐ Frequent |
| 3) | My direct report needs me or an expert occasionally when he/she encounters unusual situations. | ☐ Occasional |
| 4) | My direct report can figure out what to do and dosen't need my direction. | ☐ Never |

| | Check One |
|---|---|
| ***SKILL ASSESSMENT:*** *Use the competency chart in Fig 9.2 to evaluate the competeney in the Critical Skill.* | ☐ L1<br>☐ L2<br>☐ L3<br>☐ L4 |

FIGURE 9.1  **Competency Evaluation Form**

The level of supervision measures the level required not the level received, as a person might need supervision he does not receive and might receive supervision he does not need.

This form lists the questions to answer in the two categories. You check one of the boxes for each category. Then, you check the box at the bottom of the form that corresponds to your evaluation of the skill based on your assessment. For example, if you evaluated the "extent of effort" as high and the "extent of supervision" as high, then you would check the box L1 for the skill.

The four levels of competency on this form corresponds to the following range of the ability of the person in a given skill:

➤ L1 is a very low competency level

➤ L2 is a low competency level

➤ L3 is a medium competency level

➤ L4 is a high competency level

While this method of evaluation is subjective, it is useful in assessing competency and is consistent with the delegation process we have used in the accountability discussion in Chapter 6. When you delegate, you want the work to be done efficiently and without your supervision. You are much more willing to delegate to a person who can do the job with less effort and no supervision from you. That would be a person who has L4 competency in a skill. To improve objectivity of the evaluation and increase agreement and ownership, the individual self-evaluates, the boss evaluates, and they have a conversation to understand each other and to arrive at a consensus.

Figure 9.2 provides a chart to serve as a visual guide for conversation between you and your direct reports on their level of competency in the skill. Take your assessment from section A and B of Figure 9.1 as two points on the top and bottom of Figure 9.2 and connect the two points to determine the zone in which most of the line segment falls. This will enable you and your direct report to agree on the competency level. If the two of you decide that the level of effort is between medium and high and the level of supervision is frequent, then the diagram shows the skill to be in the L2 zone.

In most cases, when the level of effort is high, the level of supervision is also more frequent. However, there could be cases where effort is very high and supervision is very low, and the line segment may cut across zones. In this case, a conversation with your

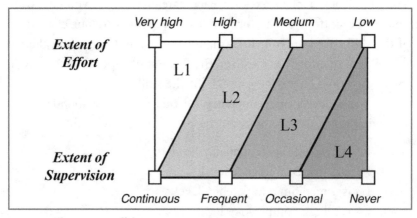

FIGURE 9.2 **Competency Chart**

boss is necessary to arrive at an agreed baseline. L4 and L3 would not apply because you can't be highly competent if you are putting in a very high effort. Regarding the absence of supervision, if you actually need supervision but your boss is not providing it, then the skill level could be L2 or even L1. The chart provides a framework for conversation as a guide for determining the level of competency.

As mentioned above, the measure of supervision is based on what a person needs, not what he or she receives. Some managers mistakenly provide continuous supervision to a collaborator who only needs occasional supervision. And some managers don't provide the supervision the collaborator needs. This should be part of the conversation.

There are two important points to remember. First, you are only assessing competency on particular skills. A person could be highly competent in one skill but might lack competence in another. You should always remember that you are evaluating the skill, not the person.

The second point is that the purpose of evaluating competency is improvement. Don't fall into the trap of spending too much time on determining which level you are in. We have seen some cases where people over analyze their present category, rather than establishing a baseline from which improvement could be made. This is not an exact science, but is a valuable point of reference to give perspective. The main point is to agree with your boss on the baseline and embark on an effective plan to improve the skill.

### *Improving Competency*

Competency improvement benefits by a three-way collaboration of the individual, the boss, and the Human Resource Department. As with accountability, it is important to clarify who has the direct impact on competency improvement and who are the stakeholders with indispensable influence.

The person with the highest direct impact is the individual. Unless the individual takes ownership of his own development, there will be no improvement in competency. As an individual, you have to want to improve and be committed. This means you will have to develop your competency improvement plan and execute the plan.

The person who can help you in developing your plan is your boss or supervisor. Besides giving you ideas, he or she can exert indispensable influence by insisting on the high competency requirements of the job. Your boss can arrange a mentor for you, someone in the organization who is more competent than you in the skill. Your boss can approve a budget for your additional training.

The third collaborator with indispensable influence on your competency improvement is the Human Resources Department. Many Human Resource Departments are charged with training and development. They have access to courses that enhance learning on particular skills. Your competency improvement plan could include some of the courses that they are currently offering, courses you need that they can design for you, or they can arrange for your training with external providers.

As we will explain in Chapter 12, a space is provided in a one-on-one conversation between boss and direct report where the topic of development is included. The purpose of that space is to agree on a competency improvement plan, and to follow up on the plan on an ongoing basis. It is in this space that the two participants decide how the Human Resources Department can assist in training and development.

## ──► APPLY IT: DEVELOP YOUR COMPETENCY ◄── WORKSHEET

Once your people have their scorecards, ask each person to begin applying the concepts from this chapter to the most important Critical Success Factors, that is, the factors with the highest weight assigned. The skills associated with improving these factors are your core skills. Let's see how it works.

### Identifying the Core Skills

Identify a core skill for each of your most important critical success factors. Here is one approach we recommend. Ask the question,

"What actions will move the status of this factor?" A good practice is for two people with the same factor or an individual with their boss to brainstorm together. This will normally generate a long list. For example, if the indicator for a sales person is "customer satisfaction index," then the question could be, "What actions will improve customer satisfaction?" The brainstormed list might look as follows:

1. Making sure that customer requirements are met by the product
2. Explaining product features to the customer
3. Communicating after sale support
4. Listening to the customer
5. Timely response to customer requests
6. Telling the truth to the customer
7. Promising only what we can deliver
8. Responding to customer rejections with courtesy
9. Improving the product the customer is buying
10. Reducing the price for the customer
11. Making the product more easily accessible to the customer
12. Ensuring that the product is shipped on time

This is a long list and not all items are under the control of the salesperson. For example, the salesperson cannot improve the product, reduce the price, or make the product more accessible. After the list is made, the individual should identify the repeatable actions that are within his control. Looking at the list above, the actions that are repeatable and within the salesperson's control are:

➤ Explaining product features to the customer
➤ Communicating after sale support
➤ Listening to the customer
➤ Timely response to customer requests
➤ Telling the truth to the customer
➤ Promising only what we can deliver
➤ Responding to customer rejections with courtesy

The theme that is associated with this list could be the title of the core skill you need. You might call it "customer satisfaction skills."

## *Evaluate and Improve*

Having identified the core skills and descriptors, here are a few additional steps you will need in order to evaluate and improve competency in the core skills.

- ➤ The individual and the boss independently evaluate each skill using the two variables, "extent of effort" and "extent of supervision" as shown in Figure 9.1 on page 109. Then they compare the evaluations, discuss the gaps, and agree on a baseline using a competency worksheet, shown in Figure 9.3. The worksheet captures all the evaluated critical skills for a person, showing the results of both the evaluation of the boss and of the self-evaluation.
- ➤ The individual develops a competency improvement plan for himself and receives the agreement and support of the boss. The plan may well include support from the HR department. Progress in competency development is reviewed in future one-on-one conversations we will be describing in Chapter 12.

The worksheet in Figure 9.3 will serve to facilitate conversation and capture agreement between the boss and the collaborator.

| Critical Skill | Assessment | | Agreed Level | Development Plan | Deadline |
| | Self | Boss | | | |
| --- | --- | --- | --- | --- | --- |
| | | | | | |
| | | | | | |
| | | | | | |
| | | | | | |
| | | | | | |

FIGURE 9.3 **Competency Worksheet**

### *An Example of a Development Conversation*

Let's look at an example of a sales manager having a development conversation about competency with one of her salespeople. A development conversation itself is a skill that requires competency. Let's first look at the descriptors for this skill:

➤ Putting the person at ease and being responsive to them
➤ Facilitating the narrowing of evaluation gaps
➤ Encouraging the person to take ownership for development
➤ Focusing on development needs
➤ Providing support for development
➤ Communicating expectations on improving competency

A sales supervisor, Amanda, is having a conversation with a salesman named Tony. Tony has a high opinion of himself, but his performance has been barely acceptable. Tony has been a continuing challenge for Amanda. Every time Tony goes on a sales call, he returns and tells Amanda what a great job he has done and how excited people were with his presentation. Yet his actual sales figures are very low. Although Amanda has worked closely with Tony over the past months and her involvement has helped his performance, he attributes the improvement solely to his own efforts.

Amanda and Tony agreed that the core skills required for Tony's CSF "dollar sales" were qualifying, writing, presenting, and closing. Amanda evaluated Tony's skill sets using the questionnaire in Figure 9.1 on page 109 as follows:

➤ Qualifying—L2
➤ Writing—L1
➤ Presenting—L3
➤ Closing—L1

Tony evaluated himself as L4 across the board. Here is how their conversation went:

"By now you have had a chance to go over my assessment of your skills. What do you think, Tony?" asked Amanda.

"I think I'm fully competent in all the skills we talked about. If you need proof, look at the sale I brought in last month. That sale brought in higher revenue than anybody else's. So, why do I need development? If you just let me get on with it, I can do fine."

"OK, let's start by comparing my evaluation with yours," responded Amanda. "How did you evaluate your writing skills?" she asked.

"L4," said Tony.

"Right. I gave you L1," said Amanda. "This shows that we have a difference of opinion. So, let's try to understand each other's point of view. Why do you think you're a good writer?"

"Well, No one has ever complained about the letters they get from me, and I really like the letters I write."

"Let me tell you why I gave you an L1 for writing. This skill requires good composition, good grammar, brevity, and focus. You spend a great deal of time composing sales letters. I've seen you sitting at your computer for hours. Yet, I've had to revise all of your letters before they went out. In some cases, I've had to completely rewrite your letters. Because you are putting forth so much effort and I need to constantly supervise your writing, I consider you to be an L1 in that skill."

Tony looked at the competency chart Jane had given them. He thought about what his boss was telling him. She was right.

"I would love to see you improve your writing skills to such a level that good writing is effortless for you. And, I want to see a letter you've written that I don't have to change. If you achieve these two objectives, then you will be L4.

"Tony, my understanding of this methodology is that it is focused not so much on evaluating you, but on establishing a baseline of where you are today so we can work together to improve. We need a plan to help you improve this skill. Do you have any ideas?"

What Tony hadn't told Amanda was that he had barely gotten through college. English, in particular, had been hard for him. He started to remember how he had argued with his teachers over his grades. He finally said, "Maybe I need to take a business writing course."

Amanda was supportive. In fact she told Tony that the company would pay for a night school where he could improve his writing skills. Amanda and Tony then started a process of competency improvement for writing skills.

### *Facilitating the Competency Process in Your Company*

The guidelines we have provided above will enable you to begin this competency process in your company. However, the best time to begin the process in your company is after your scorecards are defined and your reporting system has begun sending feedback information to your people. This way, they will be able to track how their competency enhancement plans are working and impacting the results of indicators in their Focus Reports. In Chapter 12, you will learn how this competency enhancement process can become part of what managers do on a regular basis.

---

### ➤ THE NEXT STEPS ←

---

The next chapter is about core values. It gives you a break from focusing on indicators and results. We've focused quite a bit on measuring and evaluating, which are essential pieces of the Total Alignment process. But metrics alone won't get your organization where you want it to go. Although Chapter 10 does not directly focus on results, its indirect impact is significant. We will resume our theme of laser focus on the results of scorecards in Chapter 11.

# Aligning with Values

While the team members have been focused on assigning metrics to their teams, it becomes clear to Brian that making sure those metrics align with core company values is important. You will learn how to define core values and how to translate them into pinpointed behaviors that can shape the day-to-day behaviors of people striving to improve their scorecards.

## ➤ THE CASE STUDY ◄

SEVERAL MONTHS EARLIER, when Brian was delivering the keynote speech to the crowded industry conference in Chicago, a young woman had asked him how he was planning to integrate the culture of the recent entrepreneurial acquisition with that of the group of companies. Brian had given her an answer, but her question had triggered some thoughts that kept coming back to him. The XCorp Group had grown to its current size through acquisitions. TechCorp was his first acquisition of an entrepreneurial company. Had he paid enough attention to culture before acquiring TechCorp? What about the other companies he had acquired? Brian was well aware that culture was a broad and far-reaching topic. But were there opportunities to be explored by addressing cultural issues for all of them? His dream was to have an "XCorp Way"—a distinct and recognizable culture in the group. He decided to consult with the Infoman. He texted him and invited him to meet for breakfast.

When they got together, Brian explained his thoughts. He wanted the current and future businesses to maintain the positive aspects of their culture, yet he would like to have a common culture and language among them. The Infoman told him that the alignment process that had so far been introduced would, in fact, contribute to creating the common language and culture Brian was looking for. He gave a few examples. The accountability process of pushing decision making to the lowest level; collaboration through the roles that had been defined; focus on a few factors and efforts to achieve them; and giving and receiving feedback had already become distinguishing features of the XCorp culture. There was another opportunity to complement the processes underway and to have a great impact on creating the culture for the Group. The opportunity was to revisit the core values of XCorp, maybe even redefine them, give them priority, and align people's behaviors with those values.

Brian liked the idea of having another look at the core values for the Group and could see the positive impact it would have. He knew there might be some resistance from the more numbers-oriented executives, but he was aware of the key importance of having a unified culture. He invited his top team to spend a day with the Infoman in his executive conference room.

When the team was together, the Infoman began by establishing a definition of behavior and values. Behavior is what a person says or does. Habitual behaviors are behaviors that are repeated. Values are the distinguishing characteristics of the organization that are achieved through habitual behaviors. With these definitions understood and agreed, the Infoman asked the group to think about their work environment and to identify habitual behaviors that would have a positive or negative effect on the success of their company. The group consulted and agreed on the items in Figure 10.1 on page 121.

He then asked each member of the group to confidentially assess the extent of the positive behaviors they felt were present on a day-to-day basis. They assigned a number between zero and ten to each of the behaviors and averaged them. They then took the number and turned it into a percentage. When they combined everyone's input, they arrived at 60 percent. Although this was a subjective analysis, it showed the perception of the top people in the Group and was therefore valuable. By seeing the percentage of positives, the executives realized that 40 percent of the behaviors in the group were categorized as negative. This gave those present the motivation to proceed with the rest of the exercise.

| Behavoirs That Help the Company Succeed | Behaviors That Prevent the Company's Success |
| --- | --- |
| Responding to new ideas with openness | Focusing on the negative |
| Collaborating | Acting defensively |
| Taking responsibility | Showing apathy |
| Fulfilling commitments | Introducing fear into the organization |
| Following through | Hiding the truth |
| Making decisions based on facts. | Protecting turfs |
| Reflecting on action and learning | Causing disunity |

FIGURE 10.1 **Impact of Behavior on Success**

The Infoman explained that they needed to start by identifying the core values of the XCorp Group and then to be sure that behaviors reflected those values. He went through a process with them, first consulting on core values. Once they agreed on the core values, they looked at how the values would impact behaviors and how they could align the behaviors of everyone with the values.

## ⟶ ALIGN IT: CHANGING BEHAVIORS USING ⟵ A VALUE SYSTEM

In this section you will learn a process for behavior change that you can implement in your organization. This process, equally applicable to small or large organizations, includes the definition of values as distinguishing characteristics of a company. Your values, together with your mission and vision, become the key statements that guide your organization through its growth and development in the years to come.

### A Process for Behavior Change

Behavior is observable and has an impact on others. Is it possible that some behaviors could produce results and at the same time have a very negative effect on the culture of the organization and on its customer base, or even be illegal? Absolutely. Read the news to see ample examples, from major banks abusing the rights of their customers to automobile manufacturers hiding the truth from their buyers, to companies illegally copying their competitors. Imagine the cost of these behaviors on the organization when they are caught. A major automobile manufacturer agreed to pay $14.7 billion in damages for misrepresenting an important feature of their cars to the public. This cost does not include the negative impact on its image, which will no doubt negatively affect future sales. Such a cost could put many companies out of business.

Avoiding this type of situation is obviously a top priority for your company, whether you are global or local. No one should be allowed to behave in a way that could negatively impact the organization. You might wish to do an analysis of the perception of the top team or a group of people in your organization as to the type of behaviors they are witnessing. We have developed a process that will enable you to avoid negative behaviors and promote the positive ones. It all starts with the core values.

There are four steps to this process:

1. Define corporate/company values
2. Define pinpointed behaviors aligned with values
3. Change your behaviors
4. Facilitate change in others

Let's examine each of the four steps and talk about ways you can apply them to your own business.

### Define Core Values

The first step in the behavior change process is to define your core values, those certain values that should be embraced by all the employees, managers, and directors. You can brainstorm with the top team, choose from the list we provide here, or just use this list as a guide. Here are the values the XCorp Group communicated to its employees:

➤ *Trustworthiness.* Each person working for the company should behave in a way that would earn the trust of others. As a result, our customers, employees, and stockholders will trust the company. Being worthy of trust means doing one's best and getting the job done. Also being honest, truthful, and fair, not taking advantage of others, and acting with integrity.

➤ *Service orientation.* This implies an attitude of adding exceptional value for our customers. It means that we have a focus on empathizing with the customer's challenges, exceeding their expectations, and doing it with courtesy. The intent is important and must show caring for the customer, both internal and external.

➤ *Quality consciousness.* Being quality conscious means anticipating customer expectations of the product or service they are acquiring, turning the expectations into specifications for the product or service, and assuring that the specifications are met one hundred percent every time.

➤ *Respectfulness.* Being respectful means showing respect for all relationships both internal and external and treating everyone fairly and without prejudice.

➤ *Learning.* This implies "being in a learning mode" and adopting a mindset of openness to new ideas, showing humility and not having a "know-it-all" attitude in any situation. It means encouraging everyone to innovate and take risks without fear of failure or punishment.

These values can guide the conduct of the organization and have a great impact on the relationship with customers. Alignment with values can be your company's ultimate competitive advantage.

### *Define Pinpointed Behaviors*

But how do you "align" with values? How can you determine if someone is acting in a way that is aligned, for example with "trustworthiness?" You can do it by observing their actions, not only in general ways, but watching for specific behaviors that illustrate trustworthiness. Let's refer to these specific behaviors as pinpointed behaviors. Pinpointed behaviors are, by definition, specific, observable, and verifiable. An example of a pinpointed behavior that could be characterized as trustworthy is, "completing a project by the date promised."

### *Your Behavior*

No one can claim their behavior matches up perfectly with their values, but everyone can make an honest effort to improve. Each person can examine the corporate values and identify any behavior he or she might have that is not congruent with them. Then, they can make the effort to change. Changing behaviors can be difficult and will require resolution, discipline, and perseverance.

When you resolve to change a behavior, you are on the way to self-improvement. To help you along the way, you will need feedback on how (and if) you are improving. It would be ideal to have feedback from a trusted person observing you. This person could be a friend, a colleague, or a family member. However, offering this kind of feedback could be difficult for many in a working environment, leaving you with the option of being conscious of your own progress and providing self-feedback on your own improvement. Your effort will result in positive change that will be noticed in the work environment.

### *Facilitate Change in Others*

There are many books written about behavior management that give formulas of how to trigger and reinforce a desired behavior in others. These methods can be useful but might be looked at as manipulation. The best method of facilitating change in others is setting and following your own example. Show employees and colleagues what the desirable behavior looks like, and your example will inspire them to follow suit.

The four steps we have outlined above are designed to assist the top team of any organization to align behaviors with values. You perform Steps 1 and 2 in a meeting with your executive team. Then, Step 3 is done by each of the top people. The success of your top people in Step 3 will determine their effectiveness in Step 4 and in your effort to see cultural transformation take place towards coherence with values. It's important not to underestimate the power of example in an organization of any size. People will observe and follow the behavior as exemplified by their leaders.

## ➤APPLY IT: CREATE YOUR VALUE-BEHAVIOR TREE◄

To apply the concepts in this chapter, we suggest that you assemble your team and start with the exercise described above. First, identify behaviors that could impact your company positively and negatively. Then do the confidential assessment. Hopefully your results will show a far better alignment with positive behaviors than the 40 percent misalignment illustrated by the XCorp Group. Whatever the results, the evaluation will provide the motivation for your team to pay attention to behaviors and values.

Next, follow the four steps listed above. The result of the first two steps will be the definition of values for your company. It will be helpful to give a full definition of what the value actually looks like in terms of behavior so that it is not just a platitude of "feel good" words, but is in effect a concrete guideline for behavior. Remember that pinpointed behaviors are measurable, observable, and verifiable.

Once the desired values are identified and the behaviors are defined, it is helpful to place them on a tree similar to the vision tree. Figure 10.2 is a diagram that gives an example of a value-behavior tree based on the XCorp Group values. The tree can provide clarity on the intent of the value and provides a useful framework for determining if the values are respected.

In the case study, XCorp came up with five core values. Focusing on a few core values doesn't mean other values are not important, just that only a few should be considered core. Let's look at one of the branches of this tree. Let's take the value of "trustworthiness." The three concepts XCorp considered for this value are: being trusted, being fair, and fulfilling a promise. Here are the pinpointed behaviors they defined for each:

*Being Trusted*
➤ Not providing misleading information
➤ Not hiding any information
➤ Making decisions based on facts
➤ Giving accurate information

*Being Fair*
➤ Not taking advantage of anyone
➤ Recognizing people's true worth
➤ Giving credit to rivals where credit is due
➤ Not being prejudiced based on race, status, or education

*Fulfilling a Promise*
➤ Fulfilling objectives agreed upon with relationships
➤ Fulfilling and performing commitments on time
➤ Following through and showing commitment to the company

The other values are similarly stated in Figure 10.2 on page 127. We recommend that you create your own tree, with your own definitions and pinpointed behaviors that show congruence with your values.

### An Example of Behavior Change

Here is an example of behavior change from the XCorp Group. Shirin and Andrew, two of the directors of the company, studied the value-behavior tree in Figure 10.2 and identified a few behaviors they needed to improve.

They decided to help each other align their behaviors with the values by meeting weekly for dinner to consult on ways that they could support and encourage each other's efforts. Shirin was particularly interested in the idea of "intent" in service. She thought that having a deeper connection with the customer and caring about their needs made the concept of service more meaningful.

They decided to establish a fund and pay $5 to the fund whenever they did something that would go against the new behavior they were

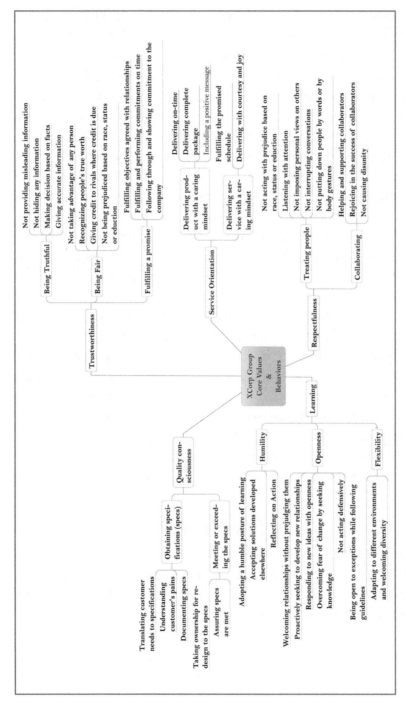

FIGURE 10.2 Value-Behavior Tree

trying to establish. If they demonstrated the intended behavior, then the fund owed them $5.

During the weeks that followed, Shirin and Andrew were in the same facility several times. They observed each other's actions. They counted the number of times each of them demonstrated congruence with the desired behavior they had selected. When they were not in the same area, each person took notes on his own behaviors and recorded the information to review during their weekly dinner meeting. Because they often reverted to their old habits, the fund became richer and richer. Yet, Shirin and Andrew diligently worked on their self-transformation process.

They had many fun dinners and outings during the weeks that followed. Suddenly, the transformation started to happen and the fund lost its cash. They continued their dinners anyway. The changes in their behavior became noticeable to others, including Andrew's boss. Their service ethic, trustworthiness, and commitment to quality earned them the high esteem of their peers.

There are elements in this example that could apply to any person. They include picking a behavior from the value-behavior tree that a person needs to change and finding a trusted person to give feedback on improvements too. In the final analysis, it is the individual's effort in self-transformation that will help him become more congruent with the company values. A support system similar to the example above will help you stay the course.

## ━━━━━━━━━━➤ THE NEXT STEPS ◄━━━━━━━━━━

In the next chapters you will be going back to the scorecards and their improvements. The next chapter is about each individual improving the results in his or her scorecard with the help of his natural team and cross-functional relationships.

**CHAPTER 11**

# Aligning for Results

The players in the XCorp case study discover that their traditional monthly results meetings are inefficient and need to be streamlined. You will learn a new approach to your monthly meetings that will enable you to improve results in the scorecards at all levels of your company.

―――――――――→ **THE CASE STUDY** ←―――――――――

BRIAN WAS HOLDING his monthly results meeting. He had asked the Infoman to sit in, observe, and give him feedback on his meeting and how it could be improved. He was concerned about the amount of time the meetings were taking, and wasn't sure if the time was well spent.

Brian began his meeting by sharing news about changes in regulations that were affecting the XCorp businesses. He talked about potential opportunities and threats; discussed the priorities for the month; and then invited each of his directors to report on the progress made in their area during the previous period. Each person gave a detailed presentation with a number of slides, charts, graphs, and figures along with comparisons against targets and with the prior year. Some of the slides were quickly passed over; others were explained in great detail. The presentations by all Brian's direct reports took a significant amount of time.

After the meeting was over, Brian and the Infoman, met to debrief. The Infoman explained that the presentation of the performance of different areas was not the best use of the valuable time of this group of high-level executives. Those present did not need to hear the amount of detail that was reported. Many seemed "tuned out" when others were presenting. The meeting didn't result in a coherent action plan. There was little real consultation. The presentations were for the most part focused on the past.

The Infoman offered a new approach to increase the effectiveness of the meeting. Rather than focusing on the presentation of each member of the team and looking mostly at data on what had already taken place, why not change the focus? Why not make the meeting upward focused and future oriented? The focus could be on Brian's scorecard and how to improve it, rather than on the scorecards of each direct report. Reference to the past would be primarily to obtain accurate data for analysis in order to make a plan for a better future.

This would mean that instead of reviewing the eight scorecards of the team members, they would be reviewing only one scorecard, Brian's. The energy of the group would be directed towards improving the scorecard of the team leader. The dynamic of the team would change from passive observers to active participants whose creative input and experience would benefit the action plans that emerge.

If Brian adopted this approach, he would gain a lot, but would be missing two types of information that could be provided more effectively in different spaces. First, he would miss reviewing the performance of each team member. A more appropriate space for this type of information would be a one-on-one meeting with each direct report. Second, his team could miss hearing important information from other areas. A short time in the agenda of the team meeting would be designated for briefly sharing relevant information that is important for the other team members to be aware of.

## ►ALIGN IT: REVIEWING TEAM RESULTS, ASSESSING ◄ OUTCOMES, AND CREATING ACTION PLANS

Meetings to review results take place in companies of all sizes. They are necessary for watching the financial and operational performance of the company and to "read the reality." But unfortunately, the vast majority of the time is spent on reporting on the past and in great detail. We are recommending that the focus of these meetings be changed from the past to the future and from reviewing the scorecards of the team members to reviewing the scorecard of the team leader. Effectively, the team reviews the Focus and Feedback Reports of the team leader in order to develop action plans for improving the team leader's scorecard. Also, on a regular basis, the team reviews the Management Report of the team leader in order to ascertain the quality of the data and goals, and to recognize good performers. The review and conversation leading to action takes place at the right level.

### *Upward Focused Teams*

The concept of teams reviewing the Focus Report of their boss and collaborating to improve his or her performance will be a huge change for many organizations. The usual practice is for the direct report to present to the boss and the team what he has accomplished in the previous period, the opposite of what we are suggesting here. The review of the team leader's Focus Report is intended not only to inform the team of what has taken place, but also to engage the members in problem solving and action planning for improving results. Figure 11.1 on page 132 is a simple diagram that illustrates the concept of interlocking natural teams that benefit by becoming upward focused.

The process that supports this approach is the "team review process." It is a process that begins with an upward-focused meeting of the natural team, produces action plans for improving results, follows the plan with action, and brings the team back together to reflect, learn, and modify the plan. We refer to the meetings as "team reviews."

Starting at the bottom of the organization, the natural team of a supervisor helps to improve the supervisor's scorecard. Then, the supervisors help to improve their manager's scorecard, and so on up the line. With this process, each person receives the creative input

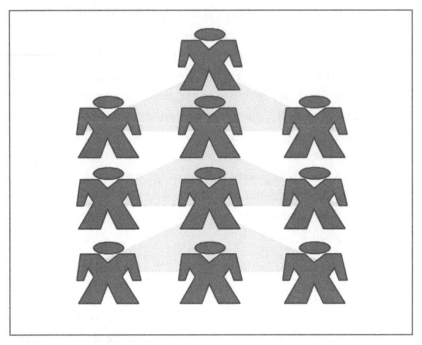

FIGURE 11.1 **Upward Focused Teams**

and support of his or her direct reports to move the indicators to the outstanding level.

### *Functioning of the Team Review*

The effectiveness of Team Review is greatly strengthened by the team having a strong and positive way of functioning. The team review has four important parts: culture, performance, development, and synergy.

### Culture

A review of one aspect of the company culture in the team review helps the team members gain a deeper understanding of the core values and desirable behaviors in the organization. The team leader chooses one value in advance and facilitates a conversation about the meaning of that value and the behaviors that should be aligned with it. The team consults about how it impacts performance. For example, the value could be "trustworthiness" and the behavior could be "delivering commitments on time." The team exchanges views related to this topic and examines how the behavior affects the performance of the team and how it would impact the value proposition for their customers.

## Performance

The main focus of the team is the performance of the team leader as reflected in his or her scorecard. This means improving the status of the factors of the leader's scorecard (Focus Report). The goal is to move all of the critical factors and initiative indexes to the outstanding level. In addition to the natural team there may be others who have a direct relationship to the factors. Who would these be? It depends on which factor in the team leader's Focus Report has been selected for action planning. If the factor is a CSF, then the additional people invited are the CIF owners for the factor. If the factor is a CMF, then the additional people are the CIM owners. (These acronyms were discussed in detail in Chapter 6. For the summary of their definition, you can refer back to Figure 6.1 on page 71.)

## Development

By development we mean the development of the functioning of the team itself. Each team has its own dynamics due to the personalities and behaviors of its members. When the members come together, the quality of their interaction will affect the outcome. Two variables can effectively measure the level of development of the team: cohesion and contribution. Cohesion means the climate of communication and unity. Contribution measures the participation of team members and the follow-through on commitments. An effective team will have high cohesion and high contribution. The conversation on development uses an assessment instrument shown in Figure 11.2 on page 134 to determine the existing level of development as a baseline for improvement. The assessment enables the team members to consult on how the team can advance to a higher level of development.

### Synergy

This is an important element of the meeting agenda. The purpose is to explore how your company can benefit by synergy between the different areas represented by the members of the team and invited guests who directly impact the factors on the scorecard of the team leader. This happens when people share relevant information from their areas and request assistance from their peers. This conversation replaces the long reports currently given in traditional results meetings. Many details that are not relevant to other members of the team are not shared.

| Team Climate (Cohesion)—Scale 0 to 10 | |
|---|---|
| Communication among team members manifest all the following: Active listening, no defensive listening, clear exposition | |
| Members show respect for each other by abiding with all the following: no put downs, no interruptions, on-time beginning and ending | |
| Arriving at consensus takes the right amount of time with: minimum repetitions, detachment from agendas, open minds | |
| There is high degree of unity among members manifested by all three: unity of vision, unity of focus, unity of action | |
| **Total for Cohesion** | |
| | |
| Team Performance (Contribution)—Scale 0 to 10 | |
| Each person is fully contributing to the consultation process by: expressing ideas, building on ideas, not being passive | |
| Each team member is fully contributing to action ensuring that: commitments are evenly distributed, there are no inactive members | |
| The talents of all team members are being fully utilized to produce results assuring that: commitments match talents, talents match the needed competency | |
| Each team member follows through with commitments to produce results such that: all commitments are done on time, deadlines don't keep changing | |
| **Total for Contribution** | |

FIGURE 11.2 **Team Development Assessment**

The four conversations mentioned above determine the focus of the team meeting. Naturally, of the four, the most important is the performance conversation as it is directly connected to the scorecards and to improving results.

## Outcomes of the Team Review Meeting

The outcomes of the team review are: commitments, action plans, and/or delta action plans. These outcomes might not emerge from each meeting. More than one meeting might be needed to gather further data for a solid action plan. Let's explore these outcomes a bit more closely.

### Commitments

Each of the four conversations in the team meeting could lead to a commitment. A commitment is an action item for a participant due by a specific deadline. A commitment should begin with an action verb and be very specific as to what is expected to take place and by what date. It is assigned to one person even though others might be involved with carrying it out. The deadline should be realistic. If later you believe that the deadline was not realistic, it can be moved with the approval of the team leader, but this should be done only before the deadline. Once the deadline is past, a commitment not completed will be overdue.

### Action Plan

The tool for improving results is the action plan. An action plan is created to improve one of the factors on the team leader's Focus Report. As explained earlier, the role for each factor also appears on that report. Possible roles are: the critical success factor or CSF, which means the team leader is the person at the lowest appropriate level of the organization who has the most direct impact on the factor; the critical influence factor or CIF, which means the team leader has indispensable influence on a factor of a peer; the critical management factor or CMF, which means the team leader has management influence on a factor of those direct reports reporting to him; and critical influence management factor or CIM, which means the team leader has dotted line management influence on a factor of a person reporting to one of his peers. To further review these roles, you can refer to Chapter 6.

How is an action plan developed to improve the status of an indicator? There is much written about problem solving that is the backbone of action planning. Some problem solving methodologies are based on root cause analysis and statistics, which you can read about if you study some of the literature on Total Quality and Six Sigma. We will highlight some of the essential features of action planning in the "Apply It" section.

### Delta Action Plan

What if the team leader has a CMF on his Focus Report that is performing below the minimum level? This shows that one of his direct reports has a CSF for the factor that isn't performing well. Should the team leader develop an action plan for this factor in his team meeting or should the team member with the CSF develop an action plan? Our answer is both, except that the team leader should not duplicate the action plan of the CSF owner. The team leader develops an action plan addressing causes within his or her control that are outside of the control of the person with the CSF. We call the action plan for the team leader's CMF the delta action plan. Delta action plans usually take advantage of the decision power, the access to resources, and the relationships that the manager has.

### *Review of Business Scorecard*

Team reviews are not intended to eliminate the quarterly review of the business scorecards. They are designed to complement, not replace them. The quarterly review is aimed at looking at the whole picture of your company's performance, while the team review is looking at the parts that make up the whole. The first is about reviewing the business scorecard and the second is about improving individual scorecards.

## Concepts to Increase Collaboration

Results are produced through collaboration, a fundamental requirement for alignment. Collaboration needs to take place both within the upward focused teams and outside the teams, throughout the organization. In particular, the action planning process requires collaboration. How do you improve collaboration? Here are two approaches: abide by the five principles of collaboration discussed below and use the team reviews to erode the silos that might exist in your organization.

### Five Principles of Collaboration

Collaboration produces a greater good, one that benefits the entire organization as well as your own department or function. The following principles of collaboration have a strong impact on releasing the power of alignment:

1. Only make a command decision when safety is at stake. This applies to everyone regardless of the role they have relating to an indicator. A command decision is a decision you take without consulting with others. In an emergency situation, a command decision could be appropriate. However, at all other times, this type of decision can be highly demotivating.

2. Only take back responsibility after it has been delegated if the person is incompetent and is being replaced. This applies to managers with CMFs. If you have a CMF in your scorecard, then you have already delegated the accountability for the indicator to someone reporting to you directly or indirectly. If you are not happy with the performance of the person who has the CSF, you should pay attention to his level of competency and put him on fast track training, or replace him.

3. Only make a decision about your own CSF after first getting input from those who have indispensable influence on your success. Every CSF owner should consult with the CIF relationships. If you make a decision completely on your own, later those with CIFs for your factor will be less inclined to help you when you need their help.

4. Only make decisions that impact the performance of people on whom you have indispensable influence after first consulting with them. This principle will help prevent CIF owners from taking over the job of CSF holders. If you have a CIF in your scorecard, and the factor is not performing well, you might be tempted to take action to solve it. But, you would be interfering with someone else's job. Your action will not only be insufficient, but it will demotivate the CSF owner.

5. If you are managing people who have indispensable influence on someone else's results, remember that their contribution should be only through influence and persuasion. This applies specifically to dotted line managers who have CIM factors. As a leader, you should encourage the people you manage to collaborate with CSF owners and not take over their jobs.

Adherence to these five principles will have a significant impact on the culture of your company and will increase collaboration. Consequently, you will witness faster execution of initiatives at all the levels and higher impact on improving results.

### Using Your Team Reviews to Erode Silos

Many organizations have developed silos. They are a type of invisible structure that impedes the cross-functional collaboration essential to alignment. Often, silos exist where one function builds its own turf without considering the needs of other functions. Silos can thrive where company politics of acquiring budget, promoting special projects, or influencing job promotions are rife. Learning about silos and how to prevent them from forming will give any company great benefits. If silos already exist in your organization, following the pattern of CSF/ CIF collaboration will help to break them down or "erode" their negative impact. Here are some of the dynamics manifested in the team review process that will help erode silos and encourage collaboration:

- ➤ As the owner of a CSF, you should know that you have permission to invite the CIF owners from different functions to your team review and consult about improving the status of your CSF.
- ➤ As a CIF owner, you know that you have permission to respond to the invitation of the CSF owner, attend his meeting and collaborate to improve a CSF.
- ➤ Whether you are a CSF owner or a CIF owner, you both share the status of the CSF, and therefore you both benefit from the improvement of the factor.

Direct communication among individuals from different departments without requiring permission or going through their boss for approval gradually erodes the silos and promotes collaboration.

## *Concepts to Encourage Creativity*

Creativity can be encouraged but not forced. In a team meeting, where people exchange ideas to arrive at a solution, creativity is of the utmost importance. To encourage creativity in this space, you should remove barriers to creativity, so that the ideas of the team members can flow naturally and be combined with other ideas to form a creative outcome. Barriers to creativity are conditions that prevent people from freely expressing their ideas. For example, you are sitting in a meeting with your peers and boss, and have an idea that you feel might be "out in left field." Should you offer this idea? Some barriers that could inhibit you from offering your idea would be: fear that your boss will reject your input, fear of losing credibility with peers, or fear of receiving negative feedback on your idea. One important way to encourage creativity is to ensure that the participants follow a code of conduct.

## Code of Conduct

We have mentioned the code of conduct in early chapters of this book. This is a very important tool for effective meetings. We are emphasizing it here to encourage creative input. Here is an example to begin with. Discuss it in your team, pick the items the team wants, or add others as appropriate. Here are some suggested guidelines for your code of conduct:

- Be on time
- Listen actively to understand, not to respond
- Participate
- No put downs
- Don't interrupt
- No hierarchy
- Be detached (offer ideas to the group and then let go of them)
- Cell phone turned off

When a team owns this set of agreed-upon behaviors, then a desired culture for the meeting is established and each member can participate freely. For example, when the guideline states, "no hierarchy," the team member has a green light to express his views even if it contradicts the views of his boss sitting in the same meeting. When the guideline states, "no put downs," the individual knows that no one will belittle him even if they feel the idea being expressed is mediocre.

### *Effective Facilitation of Team Reviews*

The code of conduct, though necessary, is not sufficient. Effective facilitation of the meeting enables ideas that are expressed by participants to merge, combine, and take shape into a creative solution. For effective facilitation, we have found that four roles are necessary: facilitator, monitor, recorder, and member. Here is a quick breakdown of each:

1. *Facilitator.* A facilitator guides the consultation; he or she doesn't direct the conversation. As a facilitator, start the

meeting on time, state the purpose of the meeting, welcome the guests (influence factor owners), introduce the agenda and the topic for action planning, and encourage the team to offer ideas and move towards arriving at creative solutions. Introduce the monitor and recorder of the meeting.

2. *Monitor.* Your role is to help the team follow the code of conduct. To fulfill this role, display the guidelines in a way that will be visible to everyone. At the beginning of the meeting, review it. Interrupt the session in real time when a serious deviation from the guidelines is affecting the flow of the meeting.

3. *Recorder.* Your role is to show software screens, Focus Report spreadsheets or other data related to the agenda, and to capture the commitments made during the meeting. There are no minutes in a team review meeting, only commitments, with individuals responsible and deadlines. Be sure to capture the decisions of the group accurately.

4. *Team member.* Everyone else is a team member. The role is to be an active participant. Arrive on time. Be in a learning mode, which means, be open to the opinions and ideas expressed by others. Offer ideas to the group without being intimidated by anyone. Take the code of conduct seriously and follow it.

The facilitator is usually the team leader, but it could rotate. The facilitator, monitor, and recorder also participate as team members in the discussion. Effective facilitation will require the individuals playing the four roles to do so naturally without considering themselves to be in a privileged position. They too must show humility and be in a learning mode. When this is the case, the barriers to creativity are removed and the meeting will be more effective.

## ⟶ APPLY IT: CONDUCT YOUR TEAM REVIEW ⟵

Team Review no doubt represents a big change from the way your company is currently functioning. To hold effective team reviews, your top executives might need training and support by a skilled trainer. Your leadership team can then cascade the concepts downwards to benefit all scorecard holders.

In the early stages of implementation, you want to make sure the concepts are correctly applied and the right habits are forming. To this end, the feedback from a coach external to the team is helpful. A coach could be doing the following: spending time with the manager to help prepare for the meeting; attending the meeting as an observer and taking notes; debriefing with the manager to give feedback.

There are many concepts in this chapter that you can apply in your own company. Here, we will focus on two areas: walk through the team review meeting and apply action planning.

## *Walk Through the Team Review Meeting*

Let's walk you through the steps for conducting your team review. We assume that you are a manager, a scorecard has been defined for you, you have a natural team of a few people reporting to you, and the system has produced the Focus and Feedback Reports for you. You decide to hold your team meeting with the new format. Below, we'll walk you through three stages: preparation, facilitation of the meeting, and follow up.

### Preparation Before Your Meeting

It is important to prepare for the team review. The time you invest in preparing will pay back many times over by shortening the meeting and increasing its effectiveness. What would you need to prepare? Here are some ideas:

- ➤ Pick a value for the culture conversation from your value-behavior tree
- ➤ Pick a CSF or CMF from your Focus Report for action planning
- ➤ Invite the CIF or CIM relationships depending on which factor you picked

➤ Perform data analysis to pinpoint the problem related to the factor you selected

➤ Have copies of the development assessment (Figure 11.2 on page 134) available.

➤ Prepare and send an agenda to your team.

**Conversation During the Team Meeting**

Your first meeting starts a new process and you want to make it the best possible experience for your team. Set aside two hours for the first meeting and pick a venue that will have the least interruptions. You might not need all this time, or you might need more time depending on the depth of action planning. Be sure there is a computer available to access information and to record the commitments that will ensue, as well as a projection device and screen to allow you to share information in real time with everyone. Be on time to set the example for your team. Here is a checklist you can use during the conversation:

➤ *Begin with the culture conversation, referring to the value and behavior you have selected.* Encourage your team members to share their understanding about the implication of the value and behaviors on their performance and on customer satisfaction.

➤ *Move to performance conversation and project your Focus and Feedback reports onto the screen.* Your team can review graphs for each indicator, study the trends, and analyze why the trend is good or bad. Explain your rationale for selecting the indicator for action planning and welcome the guests, such as CIF owners or CIM owners. Follow your company's problem-solving methodology, and pay attention to the action planning ideas discussed in this chapter to arrive at an action plan with everyone's input and commitments to implement it. The sound analysis necessary to support the action plan might need more time than allocated in one meeting. It is better to take the time to complete the action plan rather than rushing to finish within the time allotted for one meeting.

➤ *Move to the development conversation and ask your team to use the assessment instrument of Figure 11.2 to assess the levels of cohesion and contribution of your team.* The assessment should not take more than ten minutes. Ask the recorder to gather the evaluation of everyone and present the average and the standard deviation to the team. Encourage the expression of ideas by your team members on improving the team development from the baseline established through the assessment.

➤ *Move to synergy conversation.* Ask your team members to share news from their areas that benefit their peers, or request assistance from their peers, or explore synergistic topics that benefit the company.

## Follow Up After Your Team Meeting

Having developed an action plan in your meeting, it is crucial that you follow up every commitment made to ensure excellent execution. As a team leader, follow up with each person who has a task to do and be sure they are clear about what the commitment entails and that they know how to do it. Here is a checklist you can use:

➤ Carry out the commitments you agreed to do on time to set a good example.

➤ Ask your team members how they are progressing with their commitments from the team meeting and if you can help in any way.

➤ Ask your team members to send you a notice of completion of each commitment from the team meeting with a brief supporting document.

➤ Remind them to approach you (if necessary) for moving the deadline set for the commitments with the reasons, but to do this before the deadline not after.

A brief summary of the checklists presented above is shown in Figure 11.3 on page 145. You can refer to this before your team meeting each month.

How do you know if your team meeting has been effective? You know by judging the quality of the action plans that emerge, the cohesion and contribution of your team during the process of action planning, and the execution of your action plan leading to results.

| Before the Team Review Meeting |
|---|
| Determine the topic for culture conversation |
| Study your own Focus and Feedback Reports, pick a factor for action planning and invite CIF or CIM relationships |
| Have team development assessment available for the first meeting and use it for conversation about development |
| Prepare and send an agenda |
|  |

| During the Team Review Meeting | | | |
|---|---|---|---|
| Culture | Performance | Development | Synergy |
| Discussion of alignment with selected values | Presentation of your Focus and Feedback Reports and graphs | Assessment of the development of your team | Exchange of information and learning by peers |
|  | Development of Action Plan or Delta Action Plan | Review of assessment results and agreement on baseline |  |
|  | Agreement on commitments with deadlines | Discussion to improve cohesion and contribution |  |
|  |  |  |  |

| After the Team Review Meeting |
|---|
| Fulfill the commitments you made on time |
| Be available to support your team members if needed |
| Review and approve commitment done with quality by your team members |

FIGURE 11.3 **Checklist for Team Review**

## *Applying the Action Planning*

Whichever problem solving methodology you apply, we want to emphasize the importance of paying attention to the following points: pinpointing the problem, root cause analysis, solution strategy, and action plan commitments.

### Pinpointing the Problem

The problem must be defined clearly if you want the solution to work. To determine what your problem is, look at the formula for the CSF you have chosen to focus on. The formula will have one or more variables, and each variable could have sub-variables. Take each variable or sub-variable and find data on its status. Determine which section, zone, region, or which product or service is contributing to the performance of the variable that is in the formula of your CSF. If there are several areas contributing, which few areas have the 80 percent impact? Data gathering will help you answer that question. Identifying those areas with the most impact could help you pinpoint the problem.

In some cases, the problem could be in the process that is behind your CSF. For example, if your sales are down, the problem might be in the sales process or in the activities that drive the sales process. These factors must be considered as you pinpoint the problem. As the time in the team meeting is limited, this type of analysis could be done before the meeting, once you have picked the CSF for action planning.

### Root Cause Analysis

Finding the root cause behind your pinpointed problem is key to effective problem resolution. It's helpful to list the root cause and other important causes in a spreadsheet similar to Figure 11.4 on page 147. The root cause will help you solve the problem permanently; other causes will help you provide a temporary fix. Sometimes, a combination will be necessary.

| Pinpointed Problem | Root Cause and Other Causes | Impact; Low, Med, High | Within CSF Control | Within CIF Control | Within Upper Mgmt Control | External Control | Name of Who Can Act? |
|---|---|---|---|---|---|---|---|
| | | | | | | | |
| | | | | | | | |
| | | | | | | | |
| | | | | | | | |

FIGURE 11.4  **Template for Highlighting the Causes**

First, rate the causes by assigning the relative degree of impact on results: low, medium, or high. Second, for each cause, identify if it is within your control, within cross-functional control, within the control of upper level management, or if it is controlled by an external factor beyond anyone's control. Third, identify the name of the individual who can act to remove the cause. In your team meeting, you will focus on the causes listed in Columns 4 and 5 that are within the control of the team leader and the cross-functional relationships.

**Solution Strategy**

Naturally, you would focus your attention on the root cause and other causes with high impact in Figure 11.4 and develop alternative solutions, which come through a process of synthesis, of looking at the causes and pulling ideas together to address them. During the previous stage, you analyzed to find causes. In this stage, you synthesize to find a solution. This is the creative step in the process. Some people have a tendency to develop one strategy and start implementing. You should avoid that tendency and develop at least two alternatives. Also, there is a tendency to have one strategy for

| Causes | Alternative Solutions | Pros and Cons |
|--------|----------------------|---------------|
|  |  |  |
|  |  |  |
|  |  |  |
|  |  |  |

FIGURE 11.5 **Action Plan Template**

each cause. That is fine. But, the relationship of strategies to causes need not be one to one. A strategy can and should take care of several causes. Figure 11.5 can serve as a template for your solutions.

When you develop alternative solutions, you should analyze the alternatives before implementing. Do a "pros" and "cons" analysis by comparing the advantages and disadvantages of the solutions, and considering the probability of success. Determine if the solutions might have an unforeseen negative impact on results.

**Action Plan Commitments**

By "commitment," we mean a single action that contributes towards the implementation of the solution strategy. Each action will have someone responsible for it with a deadline (see Figure 11.6 on page 149). The template below gives you the columns necessary to capture the actions for follow up. Each action could be assigned to any member of your team, including your cross-functional relationships with a deadline. The commitments can be tracked, and an email mechanism can serve as reminders to the people who are responsible.

Be aware of an unhealthy tendency of teams to jump to solutions, without proper analysis, when there is a problem. It is critical to first identify the problem correctly based on data and to do a root cause

| Action Plan Commitment | Responsible | Deadline | Done |
|---|---|---|---|
|  |  |  |  |
|  |  |  |  |
|  |  |  |  |
|  |  |  |  |
|  |  |  |  |
|  |  |  |  |

FIGURE 11.6  **Template for Action Plan Commitments**

analysis. Cause and effect analysis is important because the solution developed based on such an analysis doesn't just treat the symptoms of the problem—it addresses the root cause and, therefore, prevents your problem from recurring.

## ➤ THE NEXT STEPS ◄

What you have learned in this chapter is the power of alignment for improving results. You have learned how natural teams develop and implement action plans for their team leaders. In the next chapter we will discuss the vertical review, a powerful one-on-one conversation between each individual and their boss.

# CHAPTER 12

# Coaching for Results

The Infoman introduces a new coaching process of one-on-one conversations between scorecard holders and their boss to sustain vertical alignment in the organization. You will learn the four parts of the coaching conversations for vertical alignment and how they will impact results in your company.

## → THE CASE STUDY ←

Brian scheduled his team review meeting one month after his conversation with the Infoman. Brian was aware that the new format of team review necessitated that he first hold one-on-one meetings with each of his direct reports to review the performance of each person. He asked to come to his office and brief him on the methodology for the one-on-one meetings. He also needed to understand more fully how they would relate to the overall team review.

The two discussed best practices for Brian's one-on-one meetings called "vertical reviews." This is because each manager meets with his or her team members individually for the purpose of reviewing their results as well as the action plans they have come up with during their own team reviews. Vertical reviews give managers the opportunity to coach their direct reports and help them improve their competencies. Many managers are already interacting with their direct reports frequently, but those interactions are usually prompted by the need of the moment and are not systematic or focused on the scorecards of the direct reports.

Vertical reviews help people at all levels of the company develop and become strong contributors to the vision and strategy of the organization. All individuals receive attention and assistance to improve performance through their action plans, while having the opportunity to interact with their boss one on one. The vertical reviews have the added benefit of sustaining vertical alignment in the organization.

Once Brian got some clarity on the purpose of vertical reviews, he was ready to implement using them as a step toward his coaching strategy.

## ⟶ ALIGN IT: COACHING YOUR TEAM ◄⟶ WITH VERTICAL REVIEWS

Vertical reviews, as described in the case study, are great tools for managers at all levels of the organization. They allow managers to supervise their direct reports in a systematic and organized way. Once the vertical review is finished, the manager has peace of mind because an agreement has been reached as to specific actions that need to take place. He becomes informed of performance, of plans for improvement, and the commitments of the direct report. He has the opportunity to guide and develop the individual team member.

The vertical review is also a welcome opportunity for the direct report to gain clarity on what the boss expects. Employees get agreement and support from the boss on the lines of action they are pursuing. They also receive needed encouragement and coaching on performance and competency as well as the opportunity to express any concerns.

There is great power in the vertical review process as it serves to clarify the priorities of the month between a manager and the direct collaborator. Added to the clarity of accountability the direct report has gained through the scorecards, he or she will be able to achieve results. For the manager, vertical reviews ensure that the delegated tasks are under control. This frees up considerable time to focus attention to his or her own scorecard and on future related projects for the company.

### *Vertical Review Process*

Vertical reviews support individuals to improve their scorecard performance and increase their value to the organization. The name identifies the three aspects:

1. *Vertical.* A vertical review is a one-on-one meeting between a person and his boss
2. *Review.* During the meeting the performance and competency are reviewed
3. *Process.* This is not a one-time event; it is a continuing process of improving results.

Vertical reviews start at the top level of your organization and cascade down through the levels. The CEO coaches the director and provides support and encouragement. With the attention the director receives from his or her boss, the director is supported to produce outstanding performance in the scorecard. The same happens at the next level. The director pays attention to the managers and provides support and encouragement enabling each manager to deliver outstanding performance in his scorecard. This process is repeated as shown in Figure 12.1 on page 154.

### *Coaching Opportunity*

The vertical review provides the perfect forum for coaching the next level in the organization. Just as a coach in sports strives to develop the players to win the game, the manager in the vertical review strives to develop the collaborator to achieve great performance. Since the focus of the individual is clearly defined by his scorecard, the coaching emphasis is on two objectives: improving the scorecard

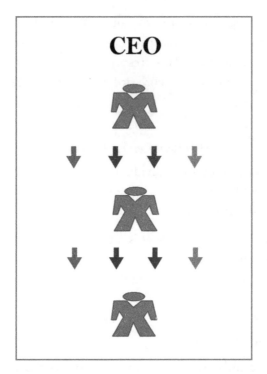

FIGURE 12.1  **Vertical Review Process**

performance and developing the talent. The manager becomes the coach and applies the appropriate leadership style to achieve the dual objective. This coaching opportunity requires attention to two important factors explained below.

### Climate of the Vertical Review

When the individual comes to meet with you, his boss, he has the natural tendency of being on guard, especially in the first meeting. He or she doesn't know what to expect and could arrive in a defensive mode. This mode affects your ability to coach. You should establish a safe environment where you can both converse and exchange ideas. Applying the code of conduct as mentioned in the last chapter will help establish the environment. Limiting distractions like cell phones is important as doing so encourages managers to take the meeting more seriously and to concentrate. Often the code of conduct will be more relevant to the behavior of the boss.

## Two Roles in Meeting

As the boss, you will act as the facilitator of the one-on one-meeting. You need to be aware of what degree of direction or support the other person requires. This can be determined partially by what skill level the person is currently functioning at. Be aware of the importance of listening. Start the meeting on time, stay focused on the purpose of the meeting, and be sure you are not interrupted by outside demands.

If you are the direct report, you will act as the recorder. You will show software screens or Focus Report spreadsheets and will capture the commitments made during the meeting. There are no minutes in a vertical review, only commitments assigned to the participants. Deadlines are also recorded.

### *Four Conversations*

Four important conversations take place during the vertical review: culture, performance, development, and miscellaneous. The manager prepares the agenda in advance and allocates time for each topic based on the priorities and needs she perceives to be important. Let's take a look at how those conversations might flow.

First, together they review the value-behavior tree (see Figure 10.2 on page 127) and identify specific behaviors that need to be improved. An example of this might be the behavior of "completing commitments on time."

Second, they review the Focus and Feedback Reports of the team member. They view the graphs for each indicator, analyze the trends in the data, and review the action plans he or she has already developed for the factors. If the action plan is aimed at the improvement of a CSF, then the manager serves as a coach to be sure the action plan fulfills the following criteria:

➤ The plan solves the pinpointed problem based on data.

➤ The plan is based on a thorough root cause analysis.

➤ Alternative solutions have been considered, and risk analysis of the impact of the solution is performed.

➤ The solution is creative and has a high probability of success.

➤ It has the benefit of the input from the individuals with CIFs who represent the cross-functional relationships.

If the action plan is aimed at the improvement of a CMF, then the manager serves as a coach to be sure the action plan is a "delta action plan" as described in Chapter 11. The review of the action plan provides the opportunity for the manager to add his input to improve the plan. Also, by viewing the cause analysis template for the action plan (see Figure 11.4 on page 147), the manager becomes aware of any causes that he can impact. The performance conversation results in specific commitments that the two participants agree on with specific deadlines.

Third, they have a conversation about competency. As discussed in Chapter 9, the core skills needed for excellent performance are jointly identified and evaluated using two variables: "extent of effort" and "extent of supervision." Here, they look at the improvement plan developed by the direct report. He gives an update on his progress in improving the skill to the next level of development. The boss adds input and provides support for the improvement effort.

Fourth, they discuss any other topic either of them considers important. It could include such topics as: vacations, changes in work schedule, progress on career path, or any other issues.

The four conversations described above can be conducted in the order listed or any order the two individuals find comfortable. We recommend that the miscellaneous topic be the last topic covered. At the initial meeting the two participants determine the frequency of the conversations. We recommend that performance and miscellaneous conversations be done monthly and the other two at least quarterly.

Ideally, the lowest level team review takes place first. Then the action plan from this meeting is presented at the vertical review of the next level before the team review of that level, and so on up the line.

## *Outcomes of the Vertical Review*

Vertical reviews have great value for both the individual and boss. The coaching translates into learning and greater focus and motivation for the person to pursue the opportunities ahead. The boss becomes aware of what is happening with the direct report and stays on top of any issues that need addressing. Other tangible outcomes of the meeting include commitments and revisions to the action plans.

### Commitments

Each of the four conversations in the vertical meeting will lead to commitments for both participants. A commitment is an action item with a specific deadline and should be clear and begin with an action verb. The participants in vertical review agree on the wording of the commitment before it is captured in the software or other tool. The deadline should be realistic. Once the deadline is past, any commitment not completed will be overdue. As the boss is viewing the action plans developed by direct reports, he may find causes that they cannot control, but he can. Commitments to address those causes will also emerge from the conversation.

### Revisions to the Action Plans

As the individual presents the action plan he has developed, the boss will have the opportunity to suggest changes to improve the plan. These suggestions should be noted by the direct report and presented in his next team review. The tendency of just going with the suggestions of the boss without discussing it in the team review should be avoided as it would demotivate the team and miss the opportunity of further enhancement of the action plan through the team participation.

## *Comparison with Performance Review*

Your company probably offers a performance review as one of your human resource processes. Managers traditionally participate in

158   ◂   TOTAL ALIGNMENT

performance reviews once or twice a year with the primary aims of setting objectives for the year and evaluating bonuses or determining salary increases. While the performance review process has value, there are some aspects that become redundant when you have vertical reviews.

The objective setting in a performance review will not be necessary as the scorecards and three goal levels replace it. The general statement of objectives of the performance review is replaced by the clarity of individual scorecards aligned with the Alignment Map. The annual report on progress toward the goals in performance review is replaced with the monthly report on progress through the Focus and Feedback and Management Reports (see Chapter 8).

The subjectivity in evaluation of performance reviews, colored by the most recent performance of the individual, is replaced by objectivity of evaluation through a system that gives due credit to the performance over the entire year. The recognition of good performance annually by the immediate boss in a performance review is replaced by the recognition of good performance of an individual monthly by all managers because of the transparency in the reporting system.

The yearly agreement of each manager with his or her boss is replaced with a more frequent monthly alignment and course correction. In the vertical review process, vertical alignment is not just with the immediate supervisor. Alignment is achieved with all the levels above and with the Alignment Map (see Chapter 5).

So, if your company has a performance review process, compare its features with the vertical review process we are presenting in this chapter, eliminate those features that are already served by the vertical review, and keep others that add value.

## ⟶ APPLY IT: IMPLEMENT YOUR VERTICAL ⟵ REVIEW PROCESS

The vertical review process is probably a big change from the way your company is functioning currently. To implement this process, your leadership team would benefit from training by a skilled expert.

The team can then cascade the concepts downwards to all scorecard holders. If you're a smaller startup and don't have the budget to bring someone in, you can apply a few tried-and-true methods. The following is an explanation of practical measures to implement these processes in your own company.

## Walk-Through for the Vertical Review

Let's walk you through the steps to follow in setting up your first vertical review. We will assume you are a manager, a scorecard has been defined for your team members, and the reporting system is in place. The system has produced the Focus and Feedback Reports for each of your direct reports. Below are the steps through three stages: before, during, and after your one-on-one meeting.

### Preparation Before Your Vertical Review

The better your preparation, the greater will be the outcome of your meeting. What would you need to prepare? Here is a checklist:

- Pick a value from your value-behavior tree (Figure 10.2 on page 127) for the culture conversation.
- Study the Focus and Feedback Report of your team member in order to determine what questions to ask during the meeting.
- Pick one core skill the person needs to improve.
- Pick any other topic you wish to discuss.

Prioritize the items above, prepare an agenda, and send it well in advance of the meeting.

### Conversation During the Vertical Review

Your first meeting is especially important. It is the introduction of a new process and you want to make it the best possible experience for both parties. Set aside an hour and a half for the first meeting and pick a venue that will have the least interruptions. You might not need all of this time, but having the time blocked off will enable you to be more relaxed and focused. Have a computer or a smartphone available to access information and record the commitments that will ensue. Be on time to welcome your team member when he or she arrives. Here is a checklist you can use during the conversation:

➤ *Try to set a relaxed and informal atmosphere.* People are often intimidated coming to a meeting to discuss their performance—especially if it is in a supervisor's office. Consider choosing a neutral location like a common conference room or even going off-site and grabbing coffee (but remember to take your laptop). You want to communicate both verbally and by your body language that the main purpose is coaching, not evaluation.

➤ *Begin with the culture conversation,* referring to the value and behavior you have selected, and reflect together on how the behavior could be manifested by both of you to impact results in your area. The message is not that you know and he or she doesn't, but that you both are exploring together how you can be more congruent with the value.

➤ *Move to the performance conversation* and ask the questions you formulated during your preparation phase about the factors, graphs, and trends in the scorecard. Ask your team member to show you his action plan, and ask questions about how it was developed. Remember the aim of looking at the action plan is not reviewing excuses, but seeking a solution. The manager's role is to review the action plan and ascertain that it was well developed. Find out if sufficient analysis was done and if the cross-functional relationships were involved. Add your input to improve the plan. The leadership style you use when asking these questions should be appropriate to the development level of the individual in the areas under discussion. The right mix of directive versus supportive style would be required.

➤ *Move to the development conversation.* If this is the first meeting, you will spend time agreeing on the core skills for her job and evaluate the level of competence. If this is the second meeting, spend time reviewing the development plan. In subsequent meetings, ask the team member to report on her progress in improving a skill you both have agreed upon from one level of development to a higher level. For example, if you have evaluated a skill as L2, you would want to know the progress in moving towards the L3 level. For a discussion of levels of competency, you can refer to Chapter 9.

➤ *For the miscellaneous conversation, ask the team member if there are topics she wishes to discuss.* Be open and attentive as you listen. As these topics are important to the other person, the attention you give to this part of the meeting will have a great impact on her enthusiasm and motivation.

## Follow Up After the Vertical Review

The commitments you discussed and developed in your meeting require a systematic follow up. As the manager, here is a checklist you can use:

➤ Honor the commitments you agreed to do on time.
➤ Determine the progress your direct report is making on the commitments you identified during the vertical review. See whether you can help in any way.
➤ Ask for notice of completion of each commitment from the vertical review with a brief supporting document.
➤ Mention that the deadline for a commitment could be only changed if it is requested with good reason and before the due date.

A brief summary of the highlights of vertical review is shown in Figure 12.2 on page 162. You can refer to this before each vertical review.

How do you know if your vertical review has been effective? The best way to determine is if the team member leaves the meeting more focused, motivated, and determined than when he entered the meeting. These are the criteria.

| Before the Vertical Review Meeting | | | |
|---|---|---|---|
| Determine the topic for culture conversation | | | |
| Study Collaborator's Focus and Feedback Reports | | | |
| Determine the topic for development conversation | | | |
| Prepare and send an agenda | | | |
| | | | |
| **During the Vertical Review Meeting** | | | |
| **Culture** | **Performance** | **Development** | **Synergy** |
| Discussion of alignment with selected values | Presentation of Focus and Feedback Reports of team member | Review of competency of core skills of team member | Conversation on topics important to team member |
| | Presentation of Action Plan or Delta Action Plan | Review of competency improvement plan for one skill | |
| | Discussion to improve the action plans | Discussion to improve the plan | |
| | Agreement on commitments with deadlines | | |
| | | | |
| **After the Vertical Review Meeting** | | | |
| Fulfill the commitments you made on time | | | |
| Be available to support your team member if needed | | | |
| Review and approve commitment done with quality by your collaborator | | | |
| | | | |

FIGURE 12.2 **Checklist for Vertical Review**

### *Support for Implementing the Vertical Review Process*

All of the processes we have described in this book serve as the foundation for the vertical review process. However, the minimum you need to start is good individual scorecards and good information. On that foundation you can build the following:

- ➤ Training on the concept of vertical review and the methodology
- ➤ Initiation of the vertical review process at the top
- ➤ Observation and coaching of the top team
- ➤ Cascade downwards

You could launch the vertical process with an orientation session at the top and then ask each member of the leadership team to go through the elearning modules to become familiar with the concepts and the methodology. To make sure the concepts are correctly applied, the feedback from a coach is useful.

In a large organization, we recommend training and certifying a team of in-house coaches who would coach managers during the first few vertical reviews and provide feedback. Often a change in the behavior of the boss is required to have effective vertical reviews. A coach can play a vital role in making sure the process is done in the right manner. If your business is smaller or a startup, you can apply these concepts across your organization and encourage employees to reflect and learn from their experience in vertical reviews.

## ➤ THE NEXT STEPS ◄

With this chapter, you have a complete picture of the alignment process and the potential impact on results. The most critical element for success is described in the next chapter—alignment of pay with performance.

**CHAPTER 13**

# Aligning Compensation

B rian examines the policies and systems in the company to make sure they don't pull people away from alignment and decides to align compensation with the scorecards. You will learn how to use the scorecards to align your bonus system and eventually your compensation system.

---

→ **THE CASE STUDY** ←

---

BRIAN WAS AT A MEETING with Ted Finely, the CFO of XCorp Group, and Gail Locke, the corporate HR director, to talk about compensation. He had become aware of a growing inconsistency in the compensation of managers throughout the group of companies. As each target company had been acquired, an even greater disparity had developed. Brian was keen to take a fresh look at compensation and come up with a plan that was consistent and fair.

Brian knew that the alignment process he had started at XCorp would definitely have a big role to play in the compensation system. When Gail made a proposal about a new scheme of compensation, Brian's immediate reaction was to get an outside perspective. They put the Infoman, on a virtual call and presented Gail's proposal to him. He acknowledged the merits in Gail's presentation and offered a few ideas she could take into consideration to enhance the scheme.

The Infoman mentioned that the extent of alignment of the individual with the vision and strategy of the company as reflected in his scorecard should play a dominant role in the compensation he receives. It would be unrealistic to expect people to take alignment seriously if their compensation is linked to some other criteria. And, alignment would be greatly undermined if the criteria that compensation is based on encourages priorities that are misaligned. However, he wouldn't recommend a drastic change overnight in compensation as salaries had been negotiated based on certain factors such as industry standards, regulation, or track records.

As it is difficult to renegotiate salaries, but easier to award bonuses, they could begin by aligning bonuses with the performance on scorecards. Furthermore, the performance in the scorecards could be considered an important factor in promotions and in salary increases. Later, scorecard performance could become the main criterion for salary adjustments and promotions.

## ⟶ ALIGN IT: INTEGRATING ALIGNMENT AND ◄—
## COMPENSATION

The main guideline you read in the story is that compensation should be linked to performance on scorecards. The results in the scorecard represent one factor, and an important one. Yet, there is another factor that is also important. It is the aligned efforts the person makes in his or her job that might not immediately translate into results. For example, when a person is training to develop a skill. This is aligned effort that might not show up as results at the time of calculating bonuses but will impact the results later. Another example is developing action plans. This also is aligned effort. However, when a person implements an action plan, the results are not immediate, and could appear months later. Therefore, at the time of the distribution of bonuses or adjustment of salaries, considering only the results represented by the performance in the scorecard would not be fair.

We are recommending aligned efforts as well as immediate results to be considered in aligning pay with performance by combining them into a number we call the 'contribution index.' How is the 'contribution index' calculated? In the paragraphs that follow we will explain the elements that could be considered in getting results and making the effort and will describe how the index is calculated.

## *Getting Results*

First, we'll take a closer look at the scorecards. Each scorecard has a mix of approximately five important factors and initiatives. Their relative weights have been established and are shown in the Focus Report of the individual in any particular month, as you read in Chapter 8. If you look at the person's results for the quarter, you would be viewing three monthly Focus Reports. As every item in the scorecard is measurable, it is easy to arrive at one index for the person's added value that combines the performance on all the factors and initiatives. Let's call this measure the "performance index."

## *Making Aligned Effort*

Making the effort is what produces the results. Efforts could be aligned or nonaligned. Naturally, you are not interested in rewarding non-aligned effort. However, aligned effort could be considered as a separate criterion because some efforts take time to produce results. It is important to encourage aligned effort to get results, not simply getting results by any means. It is this criterion that brings in the cultural aspects of alignment we have described in this book. The evaluation of the aligned effort is through an index we call "effort index." A few contributors to this index are 360 evaluations, action planning, follow-up, improving competency, and coaching to develop talent. Each of these categories is assigned a number between zero and one hundred by the individual's boss and based on solid, quantifiable evidence that the effort has been performed in a way that meets company expectations.

### 360 Evaluations

Many companies conduct an evaluation using a questionnaire. The individual is assessed by the relationships: boss, peers, direct reports, and self. It is called a 360 evaluation because it is capturing the perception of people in your circle of relationships with you at the center. The comments and scores from this evaluation help you make some necessary adjustments. This type of evaluation could be more accurately named the "360 perception metric." However, we encourage you to have a second look at your 360 evaluations process to ascertain that it does not encourage behaviors that are not aligned with the culture of alignment.

## Effort in Action Planning

Good action planning as described in Chapter 11 is key to improving results and should therefore be rewarded. By "good action planning," we mean using action plans that emerge from a sound methodology you have adopted in the company, that the right people are involved in the process, and that it actually is producing results. The metric that measures the effort in action planning is the "action plan improvement metric." It implies that the individual is developing action plans with quality based on supporting data.

## Effort in Follow-Up

Team review and vertical review generate commitments assigned to individuals with deadlines. The commitments are very specific actions that must be completed with quality by an agreed upon deadline. Any reliable tool can be used to calculate the percent of commitments the individual has delivered on time. The effort the individual expends in following up these commitments and completing them on time can be measured by "commitment follow-up metric."

## Effort in Improving Competency

Vertical review is the space where competency conversation takes place. Core skills for the individual are defined and evaluated and an improvement plan is discussed. The purpose of the conversation is to take action to improve competency on core skills. Improvement in competency is the key to the delegation of accountability and to improvement of results. The metric that reflects the effort of the individual to improve his competency is the "competency improvement metric."

## Effort in Coaching

You learned about the coaching process in Chapter 12. Coaching and developing the next level is key to strengthening the organization and talent retention. Managers need to focus not just on getting results but also on developing capacity in others. The metric that reflects the effort of the manager to improve capacity in the next level is the "team performance metric." It is a metric that combines the performance index, discussed above, of the people you manage.

## Summary of the Metric for Aligned Effort

To summarize, we described above five aligned behaviors that you could consider in the calculation of the aligned effort. They are 360 evaluations, action planning, follow-up, improving competency, and coaching to develop the next level. For each of these you can assign a metric summarized below:

- ➤ 360 evaluation metric
- ➤ Action plan improvement metric
- ➤ Commitment follow-up metric
- ➤ Competency improvement metric
- ➤ Team performance metric

Use any combination of these metrics once you have established the mechanism for their calculation. In the "Apply It" section you will see an example of the use of these metrics.

## *The Contribution Index*

Combining the "performance index" and the "effort index," you will have one overall index we call the "contribution index." How would you combine the two? First, normalize both the performance index and the effort index to a number from 0 to 1, and then apply a weighting criterion to arrive at one number. For example, you might give a weight of 80 percent to results and 20 percent to efforts. Or, you could assign 60 percent to results and

40 percent to efforts. The choice of the percentage for the degree of effort will depend on the quality of data mechanism you have set up to capture the extent of effort. The final number will be between zero and one.

### Compensation Using the Contribution Index

We recommend that you begin aligning your bonus system with the "contribution index." How do you do this? You determine the pool of bonus that is available for distribution each quarter. For example, this could be a certain percentage of your profits that can be distributed with the approval of your board. You provide the bonus either in money or intangible reinforcements such as vacation days, days off, or some other privileges.

Multiply the contribution index by the share of bonus available for the job to arrive at the amount the individual receives. For example, if you are distributing $100,000 among a group of employees, then the bonus for a person would become his share of the total multiplied by his or her contribution index.

### Mature and Developing Indicators

The scorecards will have a combination of mature and developing indicators. By mature indicators we mean those that are hard numbers that have been tracked in the company and are highly reliable such as EBIDA, $ Sales, Percent margin, ROI, etc. Developing indicators are those that do not yet have the same level of reliability. They might be indicators you are tracking for the first time. As you are aligning your compensation, we recommend that you begin to flag indictors as mature or developing, and calculate the contribution index initially with only mature indicators. At the same time, establish the criteria of how an indicator can be promoted to mature. Over time, convert developing indicators to mature and include them in the computation.

# ➤ APPLY IT: DEVELOP YOUR PERFORMANCE ⟵
## AND EFFORT INDEX

Let's take an example from XCorp Group to show you how this is applied to Arnold Turner, a supervisor in production. His performance index based on his Focus Report, for the period January to March is shown in Figure 13.1.

In this figure the indicators from Arnold's scorecard are listed in the first column. The second column shows the type of measurement, number or percent. The last three columns show the points he earned for each of the three months. The performance of each indicator is compared with the three goal levels: minimum, satisfactory, and outstanding. Depending on the status of performance, Arnold will receive a percentage of the weight assigned to the factor. For example, the first indicator, "units produced," earned him 32.7 points out of the 36 assigned to the factor as its weight. His January downtime number was higher than the maximum threshold and therefore he got 0 out of 15 available points for that factor. The performance index for the three months of this quarter were: 80.0, 94.1, and 93.3 respectively. The performance index for the quarter was therefore 89.1.

| Performance Index for Arnold Turner January to March | | | | |
|---|---|---|---|---|
| Indicators in the Focus Report | Unit | Results January | Results February | Results March |
| Units produced | # | 32.7 of 35 pts | 32.9 of 35 pts | 32.9 of 35 pts |
| Scrap | % | 19.2 of 20 pts | 19.1 of 20 pts | 18.4 of 20 pts |
| Downtime | % | 0.0 of 15 pts | 13.5 of 15 pts | 13.5 of 15 pts |
| Overtime | % | 13.5 of 15 pts | 13.7 of 15 pts | 14.0 of 15 pts |
| Products returned | % | 14.6 of 15 pts | 15.0 of 15 pts | 14.4 of 15 pts |
| Total Evaluation | | 80.0 | 94.2 | 93.2 |

FIGURE 13.1 **Performance Index Based on the Scorecard**

Now we can take a look at Arnold"s "effort index," shown in Figure 13.2. This figure shows the evaluations by his boss using hard data.

| Effort Index for Arnold Turner | | |
|---|---|---|
| Category | Metric | Score |
| 360 assessment | 360 perception metric | 75 |
| Effort in action planning | Action plan improvement metric | 50 |
| Effort in follow-up | Commitments follow-up metric | 80 |
| Effort in improving competency | Competency improvement metric | 70 |
| Management effort | Team performance metric | 85 |
| | Average | 72 |

FIGURE 13.2 **Aligned Effort Index—January to March**

The data that supports the numbers inserted in Figure 13.2 by Arnold's boss come from data capture mechanisms established in the company. Arnold's combined score for contribution index was a combination of 89.1 from his scorecard and 72 from his aligned efforts. Using the criterion of 60/40 (sixty percent for results and forty percent for effort), his contribution index would be 82.3. If the available bonus amount for Arnold were one thousand dollars, he would receive a check for $823.

The example of Arnold's bonus could apply to every individual who has a Focus Report in your company. In addition to the Focus Report, you need two methods of calculation of the results produced and efforts made similar to Figures 13.1 and 13.2. When you give a bonus based on these two factors, then the alignment of the individual is assured. He or she will make considerable effort in the five areas of Figure 13.2. They will strive to focus on the critical factors in their scorecards. The outcome is a close and desirable alignment with the alignment map, which represents vision and strategy.

### *Calculating the Contribution Index*

All of the calculations mentioned throughout this book including the contribution index can be done by using the TOPS software, which is available through our website. You can also use a combination of other software products. If you are a small company, the calculations can be done manually.

## THE NEXT STEPS

The next chapter will provide you with important tips on implementing the total alignment process in your organization.

# CHAPTER 14

# Implementing Total Alignment

Brian is aware that the positive change of Total Alignment will require his total commitment. His role as a leader is to be sure that the processes are implemented with quality. You will gain insights into the process of implementing Total Alignment in your company.

→ THE CASE STUDY ←

ONE SATURDAY MORNING Brian was sitting outside on the deck. He was thinking about alignment and how much he liked the concepts. All in all the experience so far had been positive. But as some individuals were resisting the change, he had to communicate a firm decision as to whether or not he expected everyone to adopt the new XCorp Way he had introduced.

Brian was aware that any positive change meets resistance, and the alignment process was no exception. People are more comfortable with the status quo. They have learned the rules and have figured out how to play the game. He started thinking about the benefits of alignment. He thought back to the first offsite and the unity that emerged from defining the vision of the Group. Then, there was the strategy tree and finally the alignment map. Just the task of defining these elements alone had focused his team on what really mattered. He remembered the excitement generated by those early conversations. He thought about the three reports and how valuable they were in making everyone aware of the critical factors of their jobs and how they caused people to look at their real data. Individuals would know how they are progressing against their goals and whether their factors were having a good trend.

And what about the most groundbreaking change of all—the upward focused teams and vertical reviews? The structure of these two meetings had repercussions for the way entire departments would interact with each other—working cross-functionally, giving coaching to direct reports and focusing the entire team on performance.

He thought about his desire to get rid of silos in the organization and to create a common culture and language among all businesses, to create the XCorp Way. He had already seen less attachment to silos, and even less overload of emails as people began to communicate more directly with their cross-functional relationships rather than sending emails to a large list of people.

As his mind scrolled through the many things he had learned through the off sites and training on the alignment process, he started to feel more and more convinced that this was the direction he wanted for the XCorp Group. He knew that his was a big decision. He was determined to stay the course. Total Alignment would be implemented with quality throughout the organization and he would be its champion. He decided to become the best possible role model for the methodology. He would look at every issue through the lens of alignment. He reviewed his calendar. There were a host of meetings that crowded his schedule for the rest of the month. He examined each of them to see which he could eliminate. If they overlapped with the team reviews and vertical reviews he had already scheduled, he canceled them.

Brain came across the schedule for the monthly video address he usually delivered to the top five hundred executives and managers of all the businesses of the XCorp Group. He arranged the agenda for the video address: culture of the company, performance of the company, necessity for improving teamwork, and synergies. He selected these topics to match the topics normally covered in the team review. Brian's action sent a clear message that Total Alignment was here to stay.

Nevertheless, over the next several weeks some people from the functional areas approached Brian and attempted to put doubts in his mind about the efficacy of the approach. Brian's response was kind but firm. He made them realize that this was an important initiative that was not going away. Further, he explained to them the reasons he had adopted the approach, and he assigned to them the task of learning the process and becoming one of the role models of the change he wanted to see through the implementation. He gave them a deadline to check back with him on this assignment.

## ➤ ALIGN IT: LEADING THE CHANGE PROCESS ◄

What you read in the story is the best of what we have seen in our work with organizations in several countries. Total Alignment becomes the leadership tool for the CEO. If he or she is committed to it and becomes a role model, then it will work. If the CEO isn't on board, it won't work and it should not be implemented.

Resistance to change is natural and will surface during every positive change process. It manifests itself openly or in subtle ways. People might not say that they disagree, but still work against it. They could keep introducing other approaches that, while having value, will have side effects that negatively impact the alignment process.

The following two illustrations will assist you in the implementation of Total Alignment in your company: Overcoming Resistance to Change and Examples of CEO Commitment.

### *Overcoming Resistance to Change*

Any positive change will face resistance, as people are comfortable with the status quo and have learned the rules of engagement. Here are some ideas to help you overcome their fears and inertia:

- *Knowing that the change is here to stay is the most important step in overcoming resistance.* People resisting change do so in the hope that sooner or later it will go away and they can go back to doing things the way they were before. You can overcome this resistance by affirming that the change is real. You might need to reassert this thought until resistance ends.
- *Often, people don't understand the change and the consequences it would have.* They are against it because of the fear

of the unknown. You can help eliminate this fear by increasing their knowledge about the change and how it will affect their lives positively.

➤ *You can share with people the actual benefits you feel the change will bring.*

➤ *You should communicate why the change is being made in understandable terms.*

➤ *Give people a role to play in the change process.* It could be any meaningful role. You can ask them to be a driver of the change and a role model.

### *Examples of CEO Commitments*

The example in the story comes from a real life experience of a very large client. When Total Alignment was implemented, the company had forty thousand employees. It has now grown to close to two hundred and fifty thousand. The visible demonstration of the commitment of the CEO was key to the effectiveness of the alignment process.

With another client of smaller size, once the three reports, Focus, Feedback and Management, were defined, the CEO arranged a visible show of his support by inviting the top executives into the conference room for a video shoot that would be communicated to the organization. He had arranged all the physical reports presently circulating in the company to be piled on the conference table. Then, he walked in and pushed the piles into a wastebasket. His message was that the three reports were replacing all other reports currently used in the company.

The CEO of a small client, who implemented the system manually, sent a message to all the employees by explaining that the condition for receiving their paycheck was an updated status on their scorecards and action plans. This clearly put the responsibility for producing the Focus and Feedback reports on each individual.

The CEO of another large client communicated the message to the entire organization that he was going to be the first to follow the change processes described in this book and that everyone's compensation including his own would henceforth be based on their scorecards.

## ──────➤ APPLY IT: TIPS AND GUIDELINES ◄────── FOR TOTAL ALIGNMENT

What we have presented in this book are alignment concepts to help you implement three important systems for alignment: a scorecard system, an information system, and a management system. Chapters 2 through 7 will help you implement the scorecard system. You read about the information system in Chapter 8 and the management system in Chapters 11 and 12. While inter-related, each of these three systems deliver their own distinct value. Below are some tips to help insure a successful application of the concepts.

### *The Scorecard System*

- ➤ Be sure that the indicators in the scorecards fulfill the acceptance criteria mentioned in Chapter 3.
- ➤ Be sure that people with CSFs have adequate competency to handle their scorecards. If they don't, move the CSF one level higher.
- ➤ The scorecards of the staff areas will have more CIFs than CSFs or INXs and INIs. For the definition of these terms, refer to Chapter 6.
- ➤ The scorecard of upper levels will have more INXs and INIs.

### *The Information System*

- ➤ Once the scorecards are defined, find out if you have data to support the indicators. If you have no data, or incomplete data, then focusing on data capture should be your first priority.
- ➤ If you have data, find out if it is accurate and reliable. If it is not, then improving data accuracy should be your priority.
- ➤ Setting the right three level goals (minimum or maximum, satisfactory, and outstanding) is critical because they determine the exceptions in the information system.

➤ The credibility of the information system depends on the accuracy of the data and the right goals.

## The Management System

➤ Team review and vertical review should start only after you have good data for at least one critical success factor for each scorecard.

➤ The top levels of the organization must set a good example for team review and vertical review to spread.

➤ The frequency of team review depends on the need for action planning.

➤ The frequency of vertical review depends on the needs of the direct report.

➤ When you provide the initial attention to get team review and vertical review started in the organization, work with your top performers first. Once they use the tool to improve performance, they will become your champions.

## Implementing the Entire System

➤ You need an effective strategy to implement the entire system presented in this book.

➤ We recommend paying attention first to the quality of the scorecard system, then the information system, before implementing the management system.

➤ One option is to start the first phase with one division or department as a pilot and then expand in the second phase. The advantage is that you will be able to learn and make adjustments before expanding. The disadvantage is that the top levels and the rest of the organization will have to wait.

➤ Another option is to start the first phase covering the top three levels of your organization, and move to include lower levels in the second phase. The advantage is faster alignment at the top. The disadvantage is that lower levels will have to wait and results will take longer to appear.

➤ A third option is a combination of the above: the first phase could be the top three levels and one or two pilots in a division or department.

➤ You are encouraged to customize the language we have introduced and create your "company way." Use terms that are more suitable to your culture, and choose the appropriate frequency for the conversations in your team review and vertical review.

We believe that the implementation of the concepts and tools in this book will strengthen your organization and help you produce better results. However, we make no guarantees as each company is unique and its existing culture and processes adapt to the new approach at varying speeds. Results depend on how the concepts are applied by your people. You know your own company and might wish to implement the concepts in a pilot and learn how to apply them before expanding. Keep the following two prerequisites for success in mind:

➤ The main condition for success is the commitment of your CEO.

➤ The second condition is linking compensation with performance as described in Chapter 13. Without this, people will not take the change process seriously and it will not be as effective.

## Implementation Support

If you have questions, or require support at any point in your implementation, you are welcome to contact us through our website, www.totalalignment.com/is.

We can advise you on a strategy for implementing and provide highly trained professionals to assist in facilitating, coaching and training. We can provide you with the web based software, TOPS, as well as other tools.

Distributing this book within your organization will help your people understand the Total Alignment process, and will facilitate the implementation.

## ─────────► THE LAST CHAPTER ◄─────────

The final chapter of this book discusses broader issues of alignment beyond unifying the organization behind vision and strategy. It is about aligning the vision more directly with the needs and priorities of society.

# CHAPTER 15

# A New Vision of Alignment

A near catastrophe causes Brian to re-evaluate his priorities and the goals he has set for the XCorp Group. He realizes that his plans have been missing a very important piece—looking beyond the profit motive to the needs of the society at large. You will learn some key elements to aligning with a new and broader vision.

→ THE CASE STUDY ←

JUST AS BRIAN felt like he could relax and enjoy the fruits of his labors, a crisis loomed on the horizon. Because of all of the changes made at XCorp, the group had become very attractive to investors. A hostile takeover was brewing that caused a great deal of stress for Brian and his top team. Fortunately, after several weeks of uncertainty, it did not materialize. If it had, it would have had a devastating effect. It could have taken away Brian's position and canceled the hard work he had put into the company. The stress of the threat that Brian went through had a profound effect on him. He was deeply shaken when he realized how much time and energy he had invested in building up the XCorp Group and how easily it could have been lost. He started to question the relevance of his life's work. Had his priorities been wrong? He felt more humble. He decided to consult with the Infoman about the direction his future should take and what his priorities should be.

The Infoman listened intently to Brian's thoughts and questions. He responded by bringing some principles to the conversation. He mentioned that the answers were already in place at XCorp Group and he only had to re-examine and recommit to them. He reminded him of the values they had defined together and also the vision of service that the group had consulted on.

Like most major corporations XCorp Group had given a nod to the concept of CSR (Corporate Social Responsibility), but what did that really mean? He encouraged Brian to take a deeper look at the many processes of his companies. How are their business practices affecting people's lives—not only those of the employees but also those of their suppliers? How closely has he examined the supply chain of their product lines? What about the environmental impact of their production facilities? Where are they in terms of efforts to increase utilization of clean energy? Were they exceeding their carbon footprint?

Another area to investigate was their advertising and promotion. Do any of their companies employ advertising methods that misrepresent their products or mislead their customers? What about employment practices? Do they cause hardships on families? Are they encouraging diversity including making allowances for handicapped workers? Are they employing people in other cultures where they aren't obligated to pay a living wage? There are many important issues that should be the concern of a CEO who truly wishes to make a difference and to ensure that their companies are not engaged in morally questionable or inherently unsustainable practices.

The Infoman challenged Brian to consider making his next goal the implementation of Total Alignment in a way that would align the processes of production, advertising, employment, and delivery more deeply with the needs of society and to balance the profit motive with activities that will benefit society as a whole. This could be a new business model for XCorp Group.

His conversation with the Infoman profoundly affected Brian. After the Infoman left, Brian spent hours reflecting on this new perspective. He knew that CSR was part of the alignment map of XCorp Group but were they only paying lip service? Many companies talked about all the good they were doing, but in reality it was a superficial claim with many practices that were unhealthy, unfair and hurtful just beneath the surface. He didn't want the companies of the XCorp Group to fall in that category.

The more he thought about it, the more determined he became. This was a new challenge and a worthwhile commitment for his time and energy. He realized that it would be difficult to ensure that XCorp Group was "playing its part" to help create a socially just and environmentally sustainable world. It may involve changing some production methods, even phasing out some products and procedures that were detrimental. But he knew that if he was committed, it was an attainable goal.

He wanted to make a difference—he wanted the "XCorp Way" to be an example for other companies. He had the system in place and now he had the beginnings of a broader vision. He decided to have a new focus and lead XCorp Group to achieve this new level of Total Alignment.

## ⟶ ALIGN IT: APPLYING A GLOBAL ⟵ TOTAL ALIGNMENT VISION

There are many companies that have not yet come to the realization of the importance of these issues. It is not that they don't care about them, just that these ideas have not yet taken a prominent place on their radars. Companies have a direct and profound impact on the environment in which they operate. Large corporations are very powerful and can literally have a positive or negative effect on an entire country. Until this century, it was widely accepted that profit is all a corporate leader needs to think about and plan for. But as the world shrinks into a neighborhood, it has become increasingly clear that there is a moral obligation for businesses to be socially and environmentally responsible.

### *Corporate Social Responsibility*

Corporate social responsibility or (CSR) is becoming a self-regulating mechanism that companies integrate into their business models. It enables them to monitor and ensure active compliance with ethical standards and national or international norms. The concept implies that a corporation takes responsibility for the effect that its processes are having both socially and on the environment. The reality is that harm to the environment and harm to vulnerable populations are often intrinsically linked, give the concept of responsible business practices an even greater urgency. While this concept is becoming widely accepted by businesses, the measurement behind CSR and the data to support it are still in the early stage of development. This indicator was on the alignment map of XCorp Group, but it had not received the attention it deserved.

### *ISO 26000*

Fortunately more and more companies are accepting responsibility for the effect they have on physical as well as human resources. In 2010, an international organization released the ISO 26000, which is a set of standards to help companies implement corporate social responsibility. While these standards are voluntary, more corporations are accepting the idea that there should be a balance between profit making activities and activities that benefit the society in which they operate. Many companies have now made CSR part of their business model. There are both proponents and critics of this emerging international standard. Those in favor argue that while it is a standard without adequate verification, it is also a step in the right direction, something is better than nothing. The critics argue that without adequate verification, it can serve to boost the public image of companies that are not really complying. Regardless of the merits of either argument, it is clear that with proper use and verification, it could be a giant step in the right direction.

## ───► APPLY IT: CONSIDER YOUR GLOBAL ◄─── CORPORATE RESPONSIBILITY

If you have a position of responsibility in a large company or corporation, we urge you to take this issue of corporate social responsibility seriously. Companies do not operate in a vacuum. As you become increasingly aware of the environmental and social impact of your business practices, your awareness can translate into actions that are not only beneficial but will also increase brand loyalty. We encourage you to learn more about this topic and to give it priority in your company.

If you are a small entrepreneurial company, your awareness of environmental impact and social responsibility will actually present you with an opportunity. As you create your business model, consider sustainability as an opportunity and innovate in an environmentally and socially responsible way. No doubt many of the solutions for the future will come from the creativity and innovation of new entrepreneurial firms conscious of social and environmental issues.

### The Prosperity Statement

Finally, we would like to draw your attention to an important document prepared by the Bahá'í World Center as a statement on the requirements for global prosperity. It is titled, *The Prosperity of Humankind*. It presents a global perspective about the challenges faced by humanity and the opportunities to strive for global prosperity. This document presents thought provoking concepts for solving the myriad of challenges that our world faces today. It states that the solution to the problems facing humanity requires a redefinition of certain fundamental assumptions that support every institution in society. It describes the need for applying the principle of the oneness of humankind as the operating principle. It calls for a new work ethic, for reordering priorities to address poverty, redefinition of power and authority to exercise it, and global development strategy, to name a few themes. It presents fresh perspectives on social justice, human rights, universal education, and the need for social and economic development. You can obtain a free download of this document from our website www.totalalignment.com/ps for the Prosperity Statement.

### ➤ EPILOGUE ◄

We would like to express our appreciation to those of you who have been able to follow all of the concepts and read all of the chapters of this book. While alignment is a huge topic, we have attempted to give it structure and to divide the process into manageable segments.

We have implemented the concepts expressed in this book for thousands of managers. Each client has taught us a great deal as we strove to meet their needs and to adapt to the unique challenges presented by their work environment.

Total alignment is a system and a process, and it is flexible to meet the various needs of almost any company. Small companies can take the concepts and implement them manually. Large companies will need information technology to enable them to stay on top of the flow of information needed to sustain alignment.

We appreciate your attention to this important topic and are certain that it will help your people to be aligned, focused and productive. Please share *Total Alignment* with others and visit our website to let us know how we can help you.

—Riaz and Linda Khadem

# Glossary

**Align.** Position a company to move toward a common vision and purpose.

**Alignment Map.** A map connecting the vision tree and strategy tree to vision

**Behavior.** What a person says or does

**Business Scorecard.** A scorecard that measures business performance

**Code of Conduct.** A list of desirable behaviors to be followed in meetings.

**Contribution Index.** An Index measuring the contribution of the person that combines performance and effort.

**Core Values.** The fundamental beliefs that drive an organization

**Critical Influence Factor (CIF).** A factor measuring a person's indispensable influence

**Critical Influence Management Factor (CIM).** A factor measuring dotted line management influence

**Critical Management Factor (CMF).** A factor measuring a person's management influence

**Critical Success Factor (CSF).** A measure of a person's success because of his direct impact

**Developing Indicators.** Indicators being measured for the first time and might not yet show their value.

**Effort Index.** An Index that measures a person's effort in selected areas

**Feedback Report.** A report that conveys feedback on performance against goals

**Focus Report.** Equivalent to the individual scorecard

**Horizontal Alignment.** Cross-functional collaboration

**Individual Scorecard.** A scorecard that measures the individual's performance

**Initiative Index (INX).** An index that measures the progress of an initiative

**Initiative Indicator.** An indicator that measures the progress of an initiative

**Initiative Influence Index (INI).** An Index measuring indispensable cross-functional influence on INX

**Initiative Management Index (IMX).** An Index measuring management influence on initiative progress

**Initiative Management Influence Index (IMI).** Measure of cross-functional dotted line management influence on INX

**Initiative.** An important strategic project

**Key Performance Indicators.** Business metric for evaluating important factors of success

**L1 Competency.** Very low competency in a skill

**L2 Competency.** Low competency in a skill

**L3 Competency.** Medium competency in a skill

**L4 Competency.** High competency in a skill

**Management Report.** Summary of performance exceptions of direct and indirect reports

**Mature Indicators.** Indicators that have demonstrated their value and are based on reliable information.

**Mission.** The purpose and the reason for a company's existence

**Performance Index.** An index measuring the performance in a scorecard

**Pinpointed Behavior.** Specific, observable and verifiable behavior

**Process Indicators.** Indicators that measure the outcome of processes

**Scorecard.** A document that lists the metrics of performance

**Silos.** A term that refers to departments working as separate units and not sharing information or collaborating with other departments in the same company.

**Strategy Tree.** A tree relating the vision with strategic initiatives

**Team Review.** An upward focused team meeting for improving results.

**Upward Focused Teams.** A natural team focused on improving the results of the leader

**Value-Behavior Tree.** A tree of relationships between a value and associated behaviors

**Values.** Distinguishing characteristics that guide behavior

**Vertical Alignment.** Managers and direct reports being aligned

**Vertical Review.** One on one coaching session of boss with direct reports

**Vision Tree.** A tree relating the concepts in the vision with metrics

**Vision.** A picture of success for the company in the future

# About the Authors

## RIAZ KHADEM

DR. KHADEM is the founder and CEO of Infotrac, a U.S.-based consulting firm that specializes in aligning and transforming organizations. He has over 25 years of experience in strategy deployment, performance management, leadership, and cultural transformation.

Having worked with thousands of managers during his consulting career, Dr. Khadem became aware of the many systemic challenges they faced that included: too much information, too many meetings, incompatible goals, and too much pressure to play politics in organizations constrained by silos. These and other challenges were causing people to lose focus on what really matters and diminish their ability to contribute effectively to the execution of strategy. To address them he created a new management model designed to impact execution on a day-to-day basis. Thus, the unique concepts, methodologies, and tools embedded in the model join together to align the organization at all levels and transform the way managers work.

The Total Alignment model has been implemented in organizations in several countries: the U.S., U.K., Germany, Spain, Austria, Mexico, Colombia, and Brazil, and in many industries such as manufacturing, logistic, insurance, banking, health, and retail sectors. A short list of clients that Dr. Khadem has worked during his consulting career include United Technologies, Bellsouth, Bank South, GE Capital Mortgage, Avery Dennison, Mothercare, British Home Stores, Coca Cola Femsa, Grupo Bimbo, Liverpool, Bancomer, Oxxo, Softtek, Norsan Group, Grupo Guaymex, and Benavides.

Dr. Khadem has lectured in business forums in several countries and has given plenary addresses to chief executives at major congresses in Spain, Mexico, and Colombia including CEDE (Confederación Espanola de Directivos y Ejecutivos) in Spain and WOBI (World of Business Ideas) Innovation Congress in León, Mexico.

Dr. Khadem was educated at Illinois, Harvard, and Oxford (Balliol College) and holds a doctorate in Applied Mathematics. He has held teaching and research positions at Southampton University in the U.K., Northwestern University in the U.S., and Université Laval in Canada.

## LINDA J. KHADEM

LINDA KHADEM is the vice president of Infotrac, a U.S. consulting firm headquartered in Atlanta, Georgia. With her background in Sociology and Law, she has served a dual position at Infotrac as Corporate Counsel and co-author. She oversees the company trademarks and copyrights, as well as contracts with clients and representatives worldwide. She has contributed greatly to the development of Total Alignment concepts and methodologies and has been instrumental in the evolution of *Total Alignment* from *One Page Management*.

Ms. Khadem has been the co-author of the latest pocket edition of a totally revised and augmented book, *One Page Management*, published in 2014 by Editorial Norma in Colombia. She is also the co-author of *Alineación Total,* published also in Colombia and released in 2014 and *Alinhamento Total* published in Brazil in 2013.

Along with her work at Infotrac her contributions have been in the promotion of justice. She served as secretary and then chairperson of a national organization of 180 attorneys, the Bahá'í Justice society. She has spoken at numerous conferences on the theme of justice including conferences in Atlanta, Chicago, San Francisco, and Austin. She served as the coordinator of children's classes in 11 Atlanta neighborhoods—working with the children of refugees and promoting moral and spiritual education.

Ms. Khadem was educated at the University of Illinois and Emory University in the U.S., the University of Southampton in the U.K., and McGill University in Canada. She holds a Bachelor's degree in Sociology from the University of Illinois and a degree of Juris Doctor (J.D.) from Emory.

# Index

Prosperity of Humankind,
    The (Bahá'í International
    Community), 187

Q

quality consciousness, 123

R

radar chart, 13f
ream result process, 131
recorders, 141
reports, 90–103. *See also*
    scorecards
    feedback reports, 93–94, *93f,*
        98–100, *99f–100f,* 155
    focus reports, 90–93, *91f,*
        96–98, *97f–98f,* 155
    management reports, 94–95,
        100–103, *101f–102f*
respectfulness, 123
responsibility pyramid, 84–86,
    *85f*
root cause analysis, 146–147,
    *147f*
rumors, 7

S

scorecard template, *80f*
scorecards. *See also* reports
    business, 79, 83–84, 136–137
    compensation and, 166–167,
        170, 171–172, *171f*
    individual, 79–84, *80f,* 87–88,
        *87f,* 95–96
    tips for successful application
        of, 179
sequencing concept, 60–61

service orientation, 123
*7 Habits of Highly Effective
    People, The* (Covey), 83
silos, 6, 138–139
skills. *See* competency
social responsibility, 36, 184,
    185–187
solution strategy, 147–148
Starbucks mission statement, 19,
    20
strategic acquisitions, 46–47, 51
strategic alignment, 40–46
strategic direction, 40, 41–43,
    *42f,* 46–51
strategic initiatives, 57, 60,
    62–63, *63f. See also* initiatives
strategy execution, 8–9
strategy trees, 46–51, *48f–50f,*
    *52f–53f. See also* alignment
    maps
successful initiatives, 57–60, *59f*
supervision, degree of, 108–111
synergy, 134
synergy conversation, 144
synergy mandate, 40, 43–44,
    48–49

T

team development assessment
    tool, *134f*
team leaders, 131, 133, 135–136,
    141, 144
team meetings. *See* team reviews
team members, 141
team performance metric, 169
team review checklist, *145f*